Achieving QTS

Reflective Reader: Primary Special Educational Needs

117465

KT-569-044

Achieving QTS: Reflective Readers

Reflective Reader: Primary Professional Studies
Sue Kendall-Seatter
ISBN-13: 978 1 84445 033 6 ISBN-10: 1 84445 033 3

Reflective Reader: Secondary Professional Studies
Simon Hoult
ISBN-13: 978 1 84445 034 3 ISBN-10: 1 84445 034 1

Reflective Reader: Primary English
Andrew Lambirth
ISBN-13: 978 1 84445 035 0 ISBN-10: 1 84445 035 X

Reflective Reader: Primary Mathematics
Louise O'Sullivan, Andrew Harris, Margaret Sangster, Jon Wild, Gina Donaldson and Gill Bottle
ISBN-13: 978 1 84445 036 7 ISBN-10: 1 84445 036 8

Reflective Reader: Primary Science
Judith Roden
ISBN-13: 978 1 84445 037 4 ISBN-10: 1 84445 037 6

Reflective Reader: Primary Special Educational Needs
Sue Soan
ISBN-13: 978 1 84445 038 1 ISBN-10: 1 84445 038 4

Reflective Reader
Primary Special Educational Needs

Sue Soan

LearningMatters

ST. HELENS
COLLEGE

371·91 SOA

117465

JUL 2006

LIBRARY

First published in 2005 by Learning Matters Ltd.

All rights reserved. No part of this publication may be reproduced, stored in a
retrieval system, or transmitted in any form or by any means, electronic, mechanical,
photocopying, recording, or otherwise, without prior permission in writing from
Learning Matters

© Sue Soan

British Library Cataloguing in Publication Data
A CIP record for this book is available from the British Library.

ISBN-13: 978 1 84445 038 1
ISBN-10: 1 84445 038 4

The right of Sue Soan to be identified as the Author of this Work has been asserted by
her in accordance with the Copyright, Designs and Patents Act 1988.

Cover designs by Topics – The Creative Partnership
Project management by Deer Park Productions
Typesetting by Pantek Arts Ltd
Print and bound in Great Britain by Bell and Bain Ltd, Glasgow

Learning Matters Ltd
33 Southernhay East
Exeter EX1 1NX
Tel: 01392 215560
Email: info@learningmatters.co.uk
www.*learningmatters*.co.uk

Contents

Introduction

The series

The *Reflective Reader* series supports the *Achieving QTS* series by providing relevant and topical theory that underpins the reflective learning and practice of primary and secondary ITT trainees.

Each book includes extracts from classic and current publications and documents. These extracts are supported by analysis, pre- and post-reading activities, links to the QTS standards, a practical implications section, links to other titles in the *Achieving QTS* series and suggestions for further reading.

Integrating theory and practice, the *Reflective Reader* series is specifically designed to encourage trainees and practising teachers to develop the skill and habit of reflecting on their own practice, engage with relevant theory and identify opportunities to apply theory to improve their teaching skills.

The process of educating individuals is broader than the specific areas of educational theory, research and practice. All humans are educated, socially, politically and culturally. In all but a few cases humans co-exist with other humans and are educated to do so. The position of an individual in society is determined by the nature and quality of the educational process. As a person grows up, emerging from childhood into adulthood, their social and political status is dependent on the educational process. For every task, from eating and sleeping to reading and writing, whether instinctive or learnt, the knowledge and experience gained through the process of education is critical. Humans are educated, consciously and subconciously, from birth. Education is concerned with the development of individual autonomy, the understanding of which has been generated by educational, sociological, psychological and philosophical theories.

The position of the teacher in this context is ambivalent. In practice each teacher will have some knowledge of theory but may not have had the opportunity to engage with theories that can inform and improve their practice.

In this series, the emphasis is on theory. The authors guide the student to analyse practice within a theoretical framework provided by a range of texts. Through examining *why* we do *what* we do and *how* we do it the reader will be able to relate theory to practice. The series covers primary and secondary professional issues, subject areas and topics. There are also explicit links to Qualifying to Teach Standards (QTS) that will enable both trainees and teachers to improve and develop their subject knowledge.

Each book provides focused coverage of subjects and topics and each extract is accompanied by support material to help trainees and teachers to engage with the extract, draw out the implications for classroom practice and to develop as a reflective practitioner.

Whilst the series is aimed principally at students, it will also be relevant to practitioners in the classroom and staffroom. Each book includes guidance, advice and examples on:

- the knowledge, understanding, theory and practice needed to achieve QTS status;
- how to relate knowledge, theory and practice to a course of study;
- self reflection and analysis through personal responses and reading alone;
- developing approaches to sharing views with colleagues and fellow students.

Readers will develop their skills in relating theory to practice through:

- preparatory reading;
- analysis;
- personal responses;
- practical implications and activities;
- further reading.

Special Educational Needs

The SEN Code of Practice (2001) informs every trainee teacher that they are going to be a teacher of pupils with special educational needs. However, when confronted with this fact, trainee teachers may well wonder how they will manage to obtain all this knowledge and experience before qualifying. After 25 years in the classroon I am still amazed by how much I have to learn about special educational needs. Although it is an immensely demanding area, it is also stimulating and rewarding and without a doubt will improve every aspect of your daily classroom-based practice.

SEN is such a large topic and every child's needs so different that, as long as you have the desire and openess to learn, you should feel reassured that you will be adding to your experience in this area every day of your teaching career. You will not be unsupported: the management structure in schools ensures that there is a teacher, usually the SENCO, to whom you can always go for advice and support.

This book is divided into three sections:

- principles and policies of SEN;
- working with others;
- practical applications in the primary classroom.

It will provide you with the theoretical understanding on which you can start to build and develop your knowledge and good practice. Every child deserves to have a teacher who is willing and able to try to meet their individual learning needs.

This book will help you to:

- engage the issues at a theoretical level with reference to key texts in SEN;
- explore SEN issues in the primary stage of education;
- reflect upon you own principles and development as a teacher and consider how this impacts upon your work in the classroom.

Each chapter is structured around the key reflective prompts what, why and how. Each prompt is linked to a short extract. You will:

- read a short analysis of the extract;
- provide a personal response;
- consider the practical implications;

and have links to:

- supporting reading;
- the QTS standards.

A note on extracts

Where possible, extracts are reproduced in full but of necessity many have had to be cut. References to other sources embedded within the extracts are not included in this book. Please refer to the extract source for full bibliographical information about any of these.

Author

Sue Soan trained as a teacher in Portsmouth, specialising in history and mathematics. She has since taught in East Sussex, Shropshire and Kent, first as a class teacher and subject coordinator, and for the last decade, as a SENCO in mainstream schools, a MLD Unit and a specialist EBD school. At Canterbury Christ Church University, Sue is a Senior Lecturer in Enabling Learning, Inclusion and Institutional Development. She is particularly interested in social, emotional and behavioural difficulties, gifted and talented children and children's motor development. Sue has been part of a team carrying out research into behaviour for learning for the TTA. Her publications include *Additional Educational Needs – Inclusive Approaches To Teaching* (David Fulton). She is also series editor for the *Special Needs Coordinator's File* (Electric Word).

Series editor

Professor Sonia Blandford is Pro-Vice Chancellor (Dean of Education) at Canterbury Christ Church University, one of the largest providers of initial teacher training and professional development in the United Kingdom. Following a successful career as a teacher in primary and secondary schools, Sonia has worked in higher education for nine years. She has acted as an education consultant to Ministries of Education in Eastern Europe, South America and South Africa and as an advisor to the European Commission, LEAs and schools. She co-leads the Teach First initiative. The author of a range of education management texts, she has a reputation for her straightforward approach to difficult issues. Her publications include: *Middle Management in Schools* (Pearson), *Resource Management in Schools* (Pearson), *Professional Development Manual* (Pearson), *School Discipline Manual* (Pearson), *Managing Special Educational Needs in Schools* (Sage), *Managing Discipline in Schools* (Routledge), *Managing Professional Development in Schools* (Routledge), *Financial Management in Schools* (Optimus), *Remodelling Schools: Workforce Reform* (Pearson) and *Sonia Blandford's Masterclass* (Sage).

Acknowledgements

Every effort has been made to trace the copyright holders and to obtain their permission for the use of copyright material. The publisher and author will gladly receive information enabling them to rectify any error or omission in subsequent editions.

The author and publisher would like to thank the following for permission to reproduce copyright material:

Armstrong D, *Power and partnership in education*, Routledge 1995. Reproduced with kind permission of Taylor & Francis; Armstrong F, Armstrong D and Barton L (eds), *Inclusive education – policy, contexts and comparative perspectives*, David Fulton 2000. Reproduced with kind permission of David Fulton Publishers www.fulton publishers.co.uk; Cowne E, *The SENCO handbook – working within a whole-school approach*, (2nd ed.) David Fulton 2000. Reproduced with kind permission of David Fulton Publishers www.fultonpublishers.co.uk; DfES, *Removing barriers to achievement – the government's strategy for SEN*. Reproduced with kind permission of DfES © Crown Copyright; Dyson A, 'Special needs in the twenty-first century: where we've been and where we're going', *British Journal of Special Education* 2001, 28(1). Reproduced with kind permission of Blackwell Publishing Ltd; Farrell M, *Standards and special educational needs*, Continuum 2001. Reproduced with kind permission of Continuum; Farrell P and Ainscrow M (eds), *Making special education inclusive*, David Fulton 2002. Reproduced with kind permission of David Fulton Publishers www.fultonpublishers.co.uk; Farrell P, 'Special education in the last twenty years: have things really got better?'. Reproduced with kind permission of *British Journal of Special Education* 2001, 28(1); Florian L, *et al.* 'What can national data sets tell us about inclusion and pupil achievement?'. *British Journal of Special Education* 2004, 31(3). Reproduced with kind permission of Blackwell Publishing Ltd; HMSO, *Every child matters*, The Stationery Office. Reproduced with kind permission of HMSO © Crown Copyright; O'Brien T (ed), *Enabling inclusion, blue skies ... dark clouds*, Optimus Publishing (2002). Reproduced with kind permission of Electric Word plc; Soan S, *Additional education needs – Inclusive approaches to teaching*, David Fulton 2004. Reproduced with kind permission of David Fulton Publishers www.fulton publishers.co.uk; Thacker J, Strudwick D, and Babbedge E, *Educating children with emotional and behavioural difficulties – Inclusive practice in mainstream schools*, RoutledgeFalmer 2001. Reproduced with kind permission of Taylor & Francis; Wedell K, 'Putting "inclusion" into practice points from SENC0 – forum'. Reproduced with kind permission of *British Journal of Special Education* 2000, 29(3).

Section 1
Principles and Policies of Special Educational Needs (SEN)

1 The principles of SEN

By the end of this chapter you should have considered and reflected upon:

- **why** SEN principles need to be consciously and consistently examined and evaluated in the light of educational changes in policy and practice;
- **what** role SEN has in a system that endorses and encourages inclusive practice and policy;
- **how** the principles of SEN have influenced the changing agendas in primary education.

Linking your learning
Achieving QTS: Professional studies primary phase, second edition Jacques, K and Hyland, R (2003) Chapter 12.

Professional Standards for QTS
1.8, 2.6, 3.2.4, 3.2.6, 3.3.4.

Introduction

The principles that underpin the guidance given in the SEN Code of Practice (DfES, 2001b) were first introduced into schools in January 2002 and remain in place with recent further guidance such as, *Every child matters* (HMSO, 2003) and *Removing barriers to achievement* (DfES, 2004). These principles (DfES, 2001b, 1:5:7) are:

- a child with SEN should have their needs met;
- the SEN of children will normally be met in mainstream schools or early education settings;
- the views of the child should be sought and taken into account;
- parents have a vital role to play in supporting their child's education;
- children with SEN should be offered full access to a broad, balanced and relevant education, including an appropriate curriculum for the Foundation Stage and the National Curriculum.

As a practitioner you will need to identify the factors that will influence and guide the way in which you plan, assess and monitor children with SEN in your classroom. Following on from these principles are the critical success factors (DfES,

2001b,1:6,7–8). I have placed these in a table for you to begin to interrogate the relationship between the principles and critical success factors. I will ask you to take another look at this table later on, but start by examining what each phrase is actually saying and how this impacts on your practice as a teacher.

Meeting individual needs of children with SEN	Whole school issues and organisation
1. The wishes of the child are taken into account	1. All children's needs are met
2. Views of individual parents are taken into account in respect of their child's particular needs	2. Children's SEN needs are identified early
3. Interventions for each individual reviewed regularly	3. Interventions for each child reviewed regularly
4. Assessments within prescribed time limits	4. Best practice is exploited
5. LEAs statements for individual children are clear and detailed, prescribed time limits, specific monitoring arrangements, reviewed annually	5. Special education professionals work in partnership with parents
	6. Interventions for each child are reviewed regularly
	7. A multi-disciplinary approach

You should also recognise that as you engage with issues you will begin to experience the 'plate tectonic' influences that co-exist within the SEN Code of Practice (DfES, 2001b).

Before you read the following extract, prepare yourself by reading:

- Armstrong, F (1998) 'Curricula, "management" and special and inclusive education', pp48–77, in Clough, P (ed) *Managing inclusive education – from policy to experience*. London: Paul Chapman.
- DfES, 2001b, *Special Educational Needs Code of Practice*, pp6–15. Annesley: DfES.
- DfES, 2001c, *SEN toolkit, section 1: principles and policies*. Annesley: DfES.

Extract – Skidmore, D (2004) *Inclusion – the dymanic of school development*, pp12–17. Maidenhead: Open University Press.

Developments in education policy: The Code of Practice
The major policy development in the field of special needs education in England and Wales in the 1990s was the introduction, as a consequence of the 1993 Education Act, of the *Code of Practice on the Identification and Assessment of Special Educational Needs*. This was replaced by a revised version which was issued in 2001, coming into effect in January 2002 (DFES 2001). The legal status of the Code is analogous to that of the

Highway Code: whilst it does not itself form a part of statute law, all those affected by it are obliged to 'have regard' to it:

> They must not ignore it. That means that whenever settings, schools and LEAs decide how to exercise their functions relating to children with special educational needs, and whenever the health services and social services help to settings, schools and LEAs in this, those bodies must consider what the Code says.
>
> (DFES 2001, Foreword: 5)

In England and Wales, the Code defines the essential framework of Government guidance on the treatment of children with special educational needs within which schools, LEAs and other agencies must work.

When it was first introduced, initial responses to the Code often centred upon concerns about the increased workload for teachers, and especially Special Educational Needs Coordinators, implied by the introduction of Individual Education Plans (IEPs) and regular progress reviews of all children on the school's Special Educational Needs register, including those without statements (I.C. Copeland 1997); against this, some commentators welcomed the high profile given to special needs provision in schools as a consequence of the Code, correcting the relative neglect of this issue in the major educational reforms introduced by the 1988 Education Act, particularly in relation to the National Curriculum (compare Clark et al. 1997). Relatively little attention, however, has been paid to the whole way of thinking about pupils' difficulties in learning upon which the approach of the Code is built, the assumptions and presuppositions which it embodies about the nature of these difficulties, and the way in which teachers and others should respond to them.

A number of 'fundamental principles' are set out in the introduction to the Code (DFES 2001, 1: 5), which include:

- the special educational needs of children will normally be met in mainstream schools and settings;
- the views of the child should be sought and taken into account;
- parents have a vital role to play in supporting their child's education;
- children with special educational needs should be offered full access to a broad, balanced and relevant education.

There is some continuity between the thinking which informs the Code and the central documents which defined the previous policy regime in special needs education (the Warnock Report (DES 1978) and the 1981 Education Act) in the use of the concept of a 'continuum' of needs and provision (DFES 2001, 6: 22), as there is in the conditional endorsement of a policy of integration. On the question of parents of children with special educational needs, whilst they had the right to be consulted under previous legislation, the Code considerably extended and strengthened their rights vis-à-vis the other partners in the process (especially schools and LEAs), for instance in the requirement for LEAs to make parent partnership services available, the introduction of an Independent Parental Supporter, who can act as an adviser during the statutory assessment process; and through the setting up of the Special Educational Needs Tribunal to determine appeals by parents against LEA decisions on assessments and statements. The principle of access to a broad common curriculum represents a significant departure from the previous legislative regime. Whilst the Warnock Report (DES 1978) famously held that 'The purpose of education for all children is the same; the goals are the same' (DFES 2001, 1:4), the 1981 Education Act had little specific to say about the curriculum, and the Code's explicit endorsement of the principle of a common curriculum for all marks a new policy development in the field of special needs education. If we consider these principles in their totality, however, we can see that they are articulated at a high level of generality; to explore further the 'philosophy' of special needs education embodied in the Code, it is necessary to examine the mechanisms for identification and assessment which it recommends.

The Code recommends that schools should adopt a 'graduated response' to children's special educational needs. Under 'School Action', if a pupil fails to make progress despite the usual differentiation of the curriculum, then additional intervention, including an Individual Educational Plan, should be coordinated by the Special Educational Needs Coordinator (DFES 2001, 6:50). If the pupil still fails to make the expected progress, then the school may request help from external services known as 'School Action Plus' (6:62). As a preamble to these additional intervention procedures, the Code states:

> Effective management, school ethos and the learning environment, curricular, disciplinary and pastoral arrangements can help prevent some special educational needs arising, and minimise others. Differentiation of learning activities ... will help schools to meet the learning needs of all pupils. Schools should not assume that pupils' learning difficulties always result solely, or even mainly, from problems within the young person. Pupils' rates of progress can sometimes depend on what or how they are taught. A school's own practices make a difference – for good or ill.
>
> (6:18)

Taken in isolation, this statement epitomizes the standpoint of the 'organizational paradigm' of research into learning difficulties which was described in Chapter 1, which ascribes difficulties in learning to deficiencies in school organization; certainly, the tradition has influenced the language of the Code at this point. Is the Code, then, a revision of special needs policy to bring it into line with the findings of this line of inquiry? To answer this question, this passing reference to school organization needs to be situated in the context of the machinery of identification, assessment and review which the Code sets out. If we look, for instance, for an operational definition of the terms 'special educational need' and 'learning difficulty', we find the following citation from the 1996 Education Act (1:3; original emphases):

Children have *special educational needs* if they have a learning difficulty which calls for *special educational provision* to be made for them.

Children have a *learning difficulty* if they:

(a) have a significantly greater difficulty in learning than the majority of children of the same age;

(b) have a disability which either prevents or hinders the child from making use of educational facilities of a kind provided for children of the same age in schools within the area of the local education authority;

(c) are under compulsory school age and fall within the definition at (a) or (b) above or would do if special educational provision was not made for them.

This is a re-enactment of the legal definition first introduced in the 1981 Education Act, and exhibits the same circularity that was present in that legislation: 'special educational needs' are defined in terms of a 'learning difficulty', which is in turn defined in terms of a requirement for 'special educational provision', and in terms of a 'difficulty in learning' (determined normatively by comparison with the child's peer group). Although there is a reference to provision, changeable features of school organization do not feature in the definition; rather, a local norm of educational provision is presumed, and a child is seen as having special needs if he or she requires provision which is 'additional to, or otherwise different from' (DFES 2001, 1: 3) this norm. The legal definition of special educational needs, then, contains no recognition that these needs may arise because the norm of available provision is inadequate.

The concrete procedures set out in the Code (in Chapter 4 for early education settings, 5 for primary schools, and 6 for secondary schools) are largely concerned with regulating the process of identifying, assessing and reviewing the needs of individual children with difficulties. The curriculum is encompassed in the mechanism of the Individual Education Plan (IEP), which is actuated at the 'School Action' phase of assessment, and should set out the short-term targets set for or by the pupil, teaching strategies, provision, a date for review, success or exit criteria and outcomes. The revised Code places a stronger emphasis on pupil participation than its predecessor, but the vocabulary of targets and individualized intervention still seems to carry echoes of the 'behavioural objectives' school of pedagogy, popularized originally in the work of Bloom and colleagues (Bloom 1956), which was influenced by the behaviourist theory of learning formulated by Skinner (Skinner 1957). In any event, the perspective on educational provision which is encapsulated in the mechanism of the IEP is, by definition, a highly individualized approach, in which the development of a school's response to the difficulties experienced by pupils is seen as the aggregate outcome of a multitude of independent interventions made on a case-by-case basis.

A similar equivocation over diagnosis and intervention may be detected in the Code's guidance on the statutory assessment of special educational needs, the formal process in which primary responsibility for coordinating the assessment process passes from the school to the LEA, and which may result in the issuing of a statement of special educational needs. Discussing the evidence to be considered when deciding whether to make a statutory assessment, the Code advises:

LEAs will always require evidence of the child's academic attainment in all areas of learning. ...

However, academic attainment is not in itself sufficient for LEAs to conclude that a statutory assessment is or is not necessary. An individual child's attainment must always be understood in the context of the attainments of the child's peers, the child's rate of progress over time and, where appropriate, expectations of the child's performance. A child's apparently weak performance may, on examination of the evidence, be attributable to wider factors associated with the school's organisation.

(7:38–9)

Once again, there is a clear formal recognition that difficulties in learning may be the result of deficiencies in the school rather than the deficits of the child.

However, the Code continues 'Nonetheless, attainment is the essential starting point when considering the evidence' (7:40). Having first acknowledged the need to contextualize information about the child's performance and, possibly, to problematize the curricular norms within which any difficulty manifests itself, the Code then relapses into a position in which those norms are effectively taken for granted, and attention is concentrated upon the failings of the individual pupil. The remainder of the Code's guidance is largely concerned with the coordination of the statutory assessment process, and there is little further mention of the possible influence of factors in the school's organization on the pupil's difficulties in learning.

The Code makes reference to the concept of a 'continuum' (6:22) or 'spectrum' (7:52) of special educational needs, which was first introduced in the Warnock Report, with the deliberate intention that it should replace the 11 statutory categories of handicap established by the 1944 Education Act, which had previously been used to classify children with disabilities and learning difficulties. The idea of a continuum was usually taken to signify that special educational needs might vary in severity and duration, and often that they might affect pupils of varying levels of intellectual ability. However, the Code also sets out four 'areas of need' into which children's needs are generally expected to fall, namely:

- communication and interaction;
- cognition and learning;
- behaviour, emotional and social development; and
- sensory and/or physical.

There is some tension between the notion of a spectrum of needs and this taxonomy of types of need which are candidates for a statutory statement, that is it suggests that a child's difficulty must fall into one or more of these categories if he/she is to be considered as a potential recipient of the extra resources available through the statementing process.

To summarize, we may say that the Code of Practice is imbued with a contradiction between the formal recognition that difficulties in learning may arise from factors other than the attributes of the individual pupil, including aspects of the school's organization; and the nature of the procedural apparatus of identification and assessment which the body of the Code is concerned to set out. This apparatus is constructed upon a largely individualized model of learning difficulties, in which questions of school organization disappear from the picture once the graduated assessment process has been set in motion. The focus thereafter is upon monitoring and reviewing the performance of the individual pupil within a system of provision whose prevailing norms are taken for granted. Whilst the Code never attempts to set out an explicit theory of learning or pedagogy, one of its main procedural mechanisms, the Individual Education Plan, owes much to an objectives-based model of teaching inspired ultimately by theories of learning derived from behavioural psychology. There is a risk that the system of individualized record-keeping set up by the Code may act as a straitjacket upon more creative, innovative approaches to provision for pupils with difficulties in learning which are based upon the review and development of curriculum and pedagogy across the school as a whole (Clark et al. 1997; Millward and Skidmore 1995, 1998).

Why?

Why has the government issued further guidance regarding meeting the needs of children with SEN alongside of the SEN Code of Practice (DfES, 2001b)?

When you start to tackle the complexity of this issue, there are further questions that you may need to ask and reflect upon, such as:

Why did the government not update the SEN Code of Practice instead of 'adding' another strategy? Skidmore (2004) in the extract above ably guides the reader through the SEN Code of Practice (DfES, 2001b) pointing out the significant facets of it and his views of it. He summarises his findings, giving the reader a glimpse of one or two of the reasons why the government published an additional SEN Strategy, *Removing barriers to achievement* (DfES, 2004), so shortly after the revised SEN Code of Practice. Skidmore (2004) states that woven throughout the Code of Practice are contradictions between recognising that a child's difficulties in learning may be caused by factors other than the attributes of the individual child, and the overall procedural apparatus for individually focused means of identification and assessment. Interestingly he also highlights the risks he feels that the Individual Education Plan (IEP) can have on 'more creative, innovative approaches to provision for pupils with difficulties in learning' (Skidmore, 2004, p16). Therefore in his mind many of the procedures within the IEP actually hinder class teachers from developing their skills in working with children with SEN within a mainstream class and can therefore limit the creativeness of the curriculum.

It is also worth considering that the revision of the SEN Code of Practice and the Special Needs and Disability Act in 2001 did not resolve all issues and this was demonstrated in a report published a year later by the Audit Commission (2002) entitled *Special educational needs – a mainstream issue* which illustrated that challenges still existed despite the adaptations. The Audit Commission found that:

- too many children wait for too long to have their needs met;
- children who should be able to be taught in mainstream settings are sometimes turned away and many staff feel ill equipped to meet the wide range of pupil needs in today's classrooms;

- many special schools feel uncertain of their future role;
- families face unacceptable variations in the level of support available from their school, local authority or local health services (DfES, 2004, Introduction).

Clearly the government were being told that equality of service across the country was an issue, and that time factors in receiving help and training for staff to enable *all teachers are teachers of children with special educational needs* (DfES, 2001a:5:2, 44) to be true in reality, were still prime difficulties.

One of the first paragraphs in *Removing barriers to achievement* (DfES, 2004) indicates two factors:

- the government are satisfied that for those that need a substantial amount of additional support and help, the statutory framework is adequately refined;
- that there should not be so much reliance on separate SEN structures and processes to meet the needs of individual children.

It says:

This strategy aims to personalise learning for all children, to make education more innovative and responsive to the diverse needs of individual children, so reducing our reliance on separate SEN structures and processes and raising the achievement of the many children – nearly one in six – who are considered to have SEN.

Other reasons why the move away from individual identification and assessment within a possible legal framework may be encouraged are also indicated within this section of the document:

We want parents to have confidence that their children's needs will be met effectively in school without feeling that the only way to achieve this is through a statement.

Thus the fundamental principles set out in the SEN Code of Practice have not altered, but the conflicting issues that arise from within the document about how to actually enable the support and help to be given to children in practice, has required further input and direction.

How?

How are the principles of SEN impacting on all children?

Read again the fundamental principles of SEN written at the start of the SEN Code of Practice (DfES, 2001b). I believe that these are principles that are good for all children, and the government, wishing to raise children's achievement still further, and enhance social inclusion, is attempting to improve access, engagement and participation across the board, merging all areas of education and social care into one. Difficulties and positives connected to this policy and 'vision' are discussed in future chapters. However, it is how the principles are actually put into practice that has required the Code to be 'added to' in many ways. *Every child matters* (HMSO, 2003,

2.16:28) states, *while the statutory framework provides important assurances, the processes involved can be time-consuming, bureaucratic and frustrating for parents and children alike.*

The government appear to want to move away from this way of working and provide *innovative approaches to provision for pupils with difficulties in learning which are based upon the review and development of curriculum and pedagogy across the school as a whole* (Skidmore, 2004, pp16–17). This move away from the medical approach is explicit in the change of the use of Individual Education Plans (IEPs). Norwich and Lewis (2004) found that *IEPS act as a barrier to full access to the common curriculum* and Frankl (2005, p78) writes, *any move away from IEPs based on SMART targets is an opportunity to actively engage class teachers and pupils in meeting pupil's needs together.* It could be concluded that it was the mechanics of the Code of Practice that have needed further alterations and not the general principles. Also undoubtedly it is the time required for practitioners to receive training and to gain confidence and experience that is also another important issue.

The Code of Practice sits alongside the Inclusion Statement within the National Curriculum (DfEE, 1999) with its principles of:

- setting suitable learning challenges for all pupils;
- responding to pupils' diverse learning needs;
- overcoming potential barriers to learning.

These principles conflict with the procedural aspects of the Code of Practice where the child's difficulties are focused on rather than on how the learning environment, including the teacher, can overcome the barriers to learning of individual children. However, in other sections of the Code of Practice influences from outside of the child are acknowledged and the principles of the Inclusion Statement can be positively seen and applied.

In many ways therefore the principles of SEN as detailed in the SEN Code of Practice have enabled the inclusion agenda to move forward by stimulating further discussion and debate while providing a framework of support for those in need. The SEN Code of Practice (2001), the Inclusion Statement (DfEE,1999) and the SEN and Disability Act (2001) therefore tried to support inclusion while protecting, through guidance and legislation, those children with complex learning, emotional and/or physical needs.

What?

What role does special educational needs still have in primary education?

There are those who believe that special educational needs is a term and a process that is not required any more within a system working towards inclusion. Indeed many see the term outdated and unhelpful. Thomas reports in a recent article (*TES*, 2005, 17) *One knows from talking to children that the terms 'special needs' and 'learning support' have already become derogatory.* Others see the role of special education professionals as needing to change and adapt to meet the needs not only of the children with learning differences, but also the class teachers and parents. The government detailed in the SEN Strategy (DfES, 2004, Introduction) its aim to personalise learning for all children, to make education more innovative and responsive to the diverse needs of individual children. Nevertheless it also recognised that the outline timetable for implementation of the strategy was the foundation of their *longer-term ambitions for children with SEN* (DfES, 2004, Annex). As with all developments it is the way it is achieved as well as the theory and pedagogy, that is so important to whether it is successfully and positively achieved.

Personal response

- Write down as quickly as you can four words that come to mind when you think about 'special educational needs'.
- Are these words representative of what you feel SEN means in schools today or when you were a child yourself?
- Were you considered to have 'special needs' yourself or did you know someone who had?
- How were you/they treated and taught?
- Evaluate how your personal experiences or lack of them have influenced the way you perceive special educational needs now.
- Critically reflect upon your answers to these questions and examine whether you fully support the principles of SEN as described at the beginning of the chapter, writing down the positive and negative aspects, for you, as a teacher.

Practical implications and activities

1. With a colleague take another look at the table at the beginning of the chapter.
   - Explore how many of the statements highlighted refer to the identification and assessment of an individual child's special needs and how many could apply to the majority of children within a mainstream class where inclusive practice is being developed.
   - What does this tell you about the principles of SEN as described in the SEN Code of Practice (DfES, 2001b)?

2. Examine a past lesson plan that you have actually used for teaching a whole class.
   - Did your planning and differentiation of access and task enable you to include all the class fully in the lesson and its activities? If not, why not?
   - Did you use any IEPs to support your planning and mode of teaching or was there another method you used that enabled you to be able to meet the needs of the learners within the class?
   - Do you consider the use of IEPs to be useful or not ?
   - Debate the arguments Skidmore (2004) put forward (extract on p.6) with a colleague using your experience in the classroom to support your arguments.

3. Design a diagram to illustrate how you see 'Removing barriers to achievement' (DfES, 2004) is influencing classroom practice and school structures for ALL children, including those identified with special educational needs.

   • Critically evaluate why you do or don't see these changes to be positive for all members within the school community.

   • Are there any issues that require urgent attention, in your opinion, if this government strategy for SEN is to be achieved?.

4. Examine your answers to the question above with a colleague and present a case for whether you believe the action taken or to be taken as a result of the government strategy will remove barriers to learning and achievement for children with special educational needs. (To help you do this use the timetable for implementation that is included in the Annex at the back of the SEN strategy guidance.

Further reading

Blandford, S (2005) *Remodelling Schools*. London: Pearson.

DfES, (2004) *Removing barriers to achievement*. Annesley: DfES.

DfES, (2004a) *Primary national strategy, learning and teaching for children with special educational needs in the primary years*. Annesley: DfES.

Frankl, C (2005) 'Managing individual education plans: reducing the load of the special educational needs coordinator'. *Support for learning*, vol. 20(2) 77–82.

Gibson, S and Blandford, S (2005) *Managing Special Educational Needs*, pp14–22. London: Paul Chapman.

HMSO (2003) *Every child matters*. Norwich: The Stationery Office.

Norwich, B and Lewis, A (2005) 'How specialized is teaching pupils with disabilities and difficulties?' pp1–14, in Lewis, A and Norwich, B (ed) *Special teaching for special children? – pedagogies for inclusion*. Maidenhead: OUP.

2 Legislation in SEN

By the end of this chapter you should have considered and reflected upon:

- **why** it is necessary for you to have a good knowledge and understanding of the legislation for special educational needs;
- **what** the legislation means to you as a classroom teacher with regard to planning, monitoring and evaluating individual children's needs;
- **how** you will ensure that the legislation is used most effectively to meet both the needs of the children you teach and your needs as a practitioner.

Linking your learning
Achieving QTS: Professional studies primary phase, second edition, Jacques, K and Hyland, R (2003) Chapter 12.

Professional Standards for QTS
2.6, 3.1.1, 3.1.2, 3.2.4, 3.2.6, 3.3.4

Introduction

During the last 100 years the reasons for and effects of legislation for children with special educational needs in Britain has varied dramatically depending on the political and social agenda of each era. The early part of the twentieth century, for example, saw legislation passed that continued to segregate children with disabilities from their peers. Being the responsibility of the health service the Education Authorities did not have to provide these children with an educational provision at all. In fact it was not until 1970 that legislation determined that ALL children should be the responsibility of their Local Education Authority (LEA) and should therefore be provided with an education. The last 35 years have seen further tremendous changes in where and how we teach children and young people with special educational needs.

As a trainee teacher you may not feel there is value in spending time finding out about legislation that has been superseded or indeed even reading current legislation that perhaps does not discuss your main subject area (although of course every teacher teaches SEN). I would argue, however, that it is while you are a trainee that you can build firm foundations and develop good practices. With these factors in mind this chapter will provide you with the 'Why, What and How' about SEN legislation.

It is important that you understand and know about the historical perspective of SEN legislation so that the reasons for developing specific practices further and limiting others can be considered in an informed manner. However, it is vital that you have access to and have actually read and received training/INSET on current relevant legislation. I can still go into schools where important legislation such as *Inclusive schooling* (2001), *Every child matters* (2003), *Removing barriers to achievement*

(2004) and *The Special Educational Needs Code of Practice* (2001) have often not been read by teachers. Without this knowledge and understanding you will find it hard to develop your own pedagogy in order to teach children with SEN. Imagine trying to teach a geography lesson about the British Isles without knowing what the Islands look like. Special educational needs is no different and you need to have not only the strategies and approaches at your finger tips to meet individual children's various needs, but also the information provided by the government to enable you to carry out your work most effectively. With early intervention and personalised learning as significant principles being presently developed, SEN legislation and guidance will be positive and supportive instruments in aiding you in making decisions about why certain children need specific help, by what methods you are going to proceed and how you are going to achieve this help.

Before you read the following extract, prepare yourself by reading:

- Lindsay, G (2003) 'Inclusive education: a critical perspective'. *British Journal of Special Education*, 30(1) 3–10.
- Tassoni, P (2003) *Supporting special needs: understanding inclusion in the early years*. Oxford: Heinemann.

Extract: Soan, S (2004) 'Recent legislation, additional educational needs (AEN) and inclusion' pp1–3, in Soan, S *Additional educational needs – inclusive approaches to teaching*. London: David Fulton.

> Teachers need to be prepared to teach all children, and that this should be understood as both a personal and an institutional commitment.
>
> (Mittler, 2000:133)

Introduction

This chapter will introduce the recent legislation that has been influencing educational change. It will give a historical insight into how 'special educational needs', 'additional educational needs' and 'inclusion' have evolved and how they are fuelling and directing change.

Historical perspectives

There have been many pieces of legislation passed during the last century relating to disability within the United Kingdom and they do without doubt often reflect the attitudes and beliefs of the society of that era. In the past decade many pieces of legislation have been introduced building upon preceding Acts. It is for this reason that it is necessary to be aware of the chronology of these Acts and Reports so that one has a clear understanding of how legislation has evolved. However, it is not my intention to detail all the Acts and Reports passed, but only to focus on the significant recent ones, that will help guide the reader in respect of this chapter's subject.

First, it is important to remember that it was not until the Education (Mentally Handicapped Children) Act of 1970 that ALL children were made the responsibility of the local education authority (LEA). From the Education Act of 1944 until the Act of 1970,

---

'handicapped' children 'had been the responsibility of the health service as children with a learning difficulty were considered to be impossible to educate' (Tassoni, 2003). It was as a consequence of this 1970 Act that special schools began to be built, giving many children an opportunity to receive an education for the first time.

Eight years later in 1978, what was to become a very important and influential Report for the education of disabled children was published. This was the Warnock Report (DES, 1978), written by a committee that was chaired by Mary Warnock. It is this report that suggested introducing the title of 'special educational need' (SEN) to any child needing extra support. Other key proposals included recognising the need for early diagnosis and pre-school support, the *integration* of children into mainstream schools wherever possible and the need for greater parent involvement. It was hoped that in this way children with relatively minor short-term needs would be helped alongside those with more complex long-term difficulties. Importantly it also wanted professionals to focus on children's potential and the help they needed to achieve this, rather than on their disability or condition. In an attempt to prevent the labelling of children according to their medical condition the Warnock Report introduced the terms:

- speech and language disorders;
- visual disability and hearing disability;
- emotional and behaviour disorders;
- learning difficulties; specific, mild, moderate and severe.

Many of these recommendations formed the basis for the Education Act of 1981, in which the responsibility for providing support for children with special educational needs was firmly placed with LEAs. It also introduced the 'statementing' process through which a child was given a legally binding statement of special educational needs, committing a LEA to providing specific resources for the child.

Discussion

Looking at all the proposals and terminologies introduced by the Warnock Report, how influential do you think it was in shaping future changes? Do you know of any guidance or legislation this Report may have helped to shape? Why?

The 1990s

Throughout the 1980s other sigificant education legislation was passed, but for the purpose of this chapter the next significant Education Act was passed in 1993 (section 160), and was consolidated in the Education Act of 1996 (section 316) when:

the general principle that children with special educational needs should – where this is what parents wanted – normally be educated at mainstream schools was enshrined into law.

(DfES, 2001a)

Also it was in 1994 that the *Salamanca Statement* was drawn up at a United Nations Education, Scientific and Cultural Organisation (UNESCO) world conference in Spain. It called upon all governments, including the supportive United Kingdom government '[to] adopt as a matter of law or policy the principle of inclusive education, enrolling all children in regular schools, unless there are compelling reasons for doing otherwise' (DfES, 2001b).

This appears to have been the catalyst for the evolving changes that have been, and are continuing to be, introduced to practitioners and schools through government legislation and guidance. A Green Paper, *Excellence for All Children: Meeting Special Educational Needs* (DEE, 1997) set out a strategy to improve standards for children with special educational needs and promoted greater inclusion. This Green Paper indicates support both for inclusion and for special schools:

> There are strong educational, as well as social and moral grounds for educating children with special educational needs with their peers. We aim to increase the level and quality of inclusion within the mainstream schools, while protecting and enhancing specialist provision for those who need it.
>
> (Croll and Moses, 2000: 1)

The twenty-first century

In 2001 'The Special Educational Needs and Disability Act' (TSO, 2001) amended the Education Act of 1996 and transformed the statutory framework for inclusion into a positive endorsement of inclusion. Quickly following this was *Inclusive Schooling* (DfES, 2001b) and this document is vital for practitioners as it is *statutory guidance*, unlike the Special Educational Needs Codes of Practice (DfE, 1994, DfES, 2001a), and provides practical advice on the operation of the new inclusion framework. Being a statutory document the 'guidance must not be ignored' (DfES, 2001b: 2). Thus, it can be seen how determined the government are to make educational settings inclusive; perhaps as a step towards creating an inclusive society? Most recently the Green Paper, *Every Child Matters* (HMSO, 2003: 9) takes a further step forward, by illustrating how the government intends to integrate the education, health and social services for children, 'within a single organisational focus', 'to achieve better outcomes for children and young people' (ibid.: 69, 5.7). Undoubtedly there will be more legislation within the next few years 'to ensure the barriers to integration are removed' (ibid.: 79, 5.53) as the Green Paper states: 'We therefore intend to legislate at the earliest opportunity in relation to the above proposals' (ibid.: 79, 5.53).

What?

What are the most significant pieces of legislation?

- The Education Act, 1970.
- The report of the *Committee of enquiry into the education of handicapped children and young people* (The Warnock Report) 1978.
- *The Salamanca Statement*, 1994.
- *The Special Educational Needs Code of Practice*, 1994.
- The Education Act, 1996.
- *Excellence for all children: meeting special educational needs*, 1997.

- *The Special Needs Code of Practice*, 2001.
- The Special Educational Needs and Disability Act, 2001.
- *Inclusive schooling*, 2001.
- *Every child matters*, 2003.
- *Removing barriers to achievement – the government's strategy for SEN*, 2004.

Why?

Why are these so important?

It is important for you to know the policies that underpin practice in schools. These clearly show how the changing view of 'disability', 'SEN' and 'community' in society has evolved during the past 35 years. From these you can see, for example, that 'inclusion' has not just appeared as a recent 'government brain wave', but can be seen in an embryonic form as far back as 1978. The impact of society trying to develop systems that provide equality of opportunity and access for all individuals can also be followed through the published SEN legislation and guidance. To be able to teach in a way that encompasses all these facets you will need to have a good understanding of what the guidance and documentation are actually trying to achieve for children as individuals. Without this you will be unable to engage in the daily organisation and planning of a classroom effectively with regard to current curriculum, behaviour and social requirements. With diverse needs in the majority of mainstream primary classrooms, practitioners are required to plan and teach in a manner that enables effective learning for all. Without the knowledge, understanding and the ability to translate the theory and policy into practice these daily tasks quickly become difficult to implement and to manage. The first significant international agreement supporting inclusive education, The Salamanca Statement (UNESCO, 1994) provides within paragraph 2, the key statement of belief, five clauses which demonstrate clearly the view of children's rights that if not known can leave teachers without the understanding of where the principles and practices of inclusion originated from. They are:

- every child has a fundamental right to education, and must be given the opportunity to achieve and maintain an acceptable level of learning;
- every child has unique characteristics, interests, abilities and learning needs;
- education systems should be designed and educational programmes implemented to take into account the wide diversity of these characteristics and needs;
- those with special educational needs must have access to regular schools which should accommodate them within a child-centred pedagogy capable of meeting these needs;
- regular schools with this inclusive orientation are the most effective measures of combating decimator attitudes, creating welcoming communities, building an inclusive society and achieving education for all; moreover, they provide an effective education to the majority of children and improve the efficiency and ultimately the cost-effectiveness of the entire education system. (Lindsay, G (2003) 'Inclusive Education: a critical perspective,' *British Journal of Special Education*, 30(1) 3–12).

Much critical debate has taken place and is still taking place concerning these clauses, and about the conceptual and practical issues of inclusion, but if a practitioner is unaware of such significant policy their ability to teach in an inclusive way is lacking in a conceptual framework. This would also question whether they had the theoretical understanding to move thinking forward in their schools, in an informed manner.

How?

How can legislation help you in the classroom?

Every child matters (2003) clearly identifies the way the government intends to develop children's services across England and Wales. If you, as a teacher, are unaware of this Green Paper, you might not know that you could ask your SENCO or inclusion manager to help with issues for a child with SEN that requires skills from either the health service or social services. Factors such as how to enable a TA to aid an individual child and your role in this as a class teacher, can also be found in recent legislation (DfES, 2004) providing facts you can actually produce if you wish to make changes that perhaps are not too popular. The legislation, *Inclusive schooling*, (DfES, 2001a) provides statutory guidance on what are 'reasonable steps' for a school and teachers to take in changing their practices to enable a pupil to have access to and participation and engagement in the curriculum and social life of the community. With this in mind at all times practitioners will be able to include strategies and interventions into their lesson plans that will foster and promote both inclusive theory and policy while bearing in mind the needs of all pupils in the class. *Removing barriers to achievement* (DfES, 2004) provides information that when transferred into practice supports the teacher in planning and teaching pupils with special educational needs. It supports the cutting down of bureaucracy and paperwork for classroom teachers, such as the writing of IEPs for every pupil on the SEN register. The significance of documentation in supporting practice therefore should not be underestimated.

Personal response

If you were given the opportunity to present to all your colleagues across England and Wales one piece of new legislation you would like to see implemented to aid and support pupils with SEN:

- What would it be?
- How would you get your colleagues to read it and to actually implement it into their daily planning and practice?

Practical implications and activities

1. What piece of legislation or guidance from the ones below do you think would be the most helpful to you as a class teacher and why? Explore your responses with a colleague.
   - *The Special Educational Needs Code of Practice, 2001*
   - *Inclusive schooling, 2001*
   - *The National Special Educational Needs Specialist Standards, 1999*
   - *Every child matters, 2003*
   - *Removing barriers to achievement – the government's strategy for SEN, 2004.*

Take time to read these documents and to consider in detail how they would help you (a) as a reflective class teacher and (b) as part of a school team. Write positive comments for (a) and (b) on a simple chart and then see which piece of legislation/guidance should be on your shelf at school all of the time.

Further reading

Armstrong, F (1998) 'Curricula, "management" and special and inclusive education', in Clough, P (ed) *Managing inclusive education – from policy to experience.* London: Paul Chapman Publishers Ltd.

Blandford, S (2005) *Remodelling in schools: workforce reform.* London: Pearson.

Farrell, M (2001) *Standards and special educational needs.* London: Continuum.

Lindsay, G (2003) 'Inclusive education: a critical perspective'. *British Journal of Special Education*, 30(1): 3–12.

O'Brien, T (2001) *Enabling inclusion: blue skies.......dark clouds?* London: Optimus Publishing.

UNESCO (1994) *The UNESCO Salamanca Statement and framework for action on special needs education.* Paris: UNESCO.

Before you read the next extract prepare yourself by reading:

- DfES, *The Special Educational Needs Code of Practice*, (2001). Annesley: DfES. Chapters 2 and 3.
- HMSO, *Every child matters*, (2003). Norwich: The Stationery Office.

And look at:

www.ioe.ac.uk/projects/eppe

www.teachernet.gov.uk/sen

www.teachernet.gov.uk/accessibleschools

www.standards.dfes.gov.uk/studysupport

Extract: *Removing barriers to achievement – the government's strategy for SEN* (2004). Annesley: DfES. Read: The Introduction: 'Where we want to be in the classroom'.

Where we are

The 1997 Green Paper *Excellence for all Children: Meeting Special Educational Needs*[2] and the subsequent *Programme of Action*[3] published in October 1998 made a commitment to improving the statutory framework and procedures for SEN, building on experience and best practice. This commitment was taken forward through the Special Educational Needs and Disability Act 2001 and the publication of a new Special Educational Needs Code of Practice[4].

However, the Audit Commission's report *Special Educational Needs – a mainstream issue*[5] (2002) highlighted a number of continuing challenges:

- too many children wait for too long to have their needs met
- children who should be able to be taught in mainstream settings are sometimes turned away and many staff feel ill equipped to meet the wide range of pupil needs in today's classrooms
- many special schools feel uncertain of their future role
- families face unacceptable variations in the level of support available from their school, local authority or local health services.

Where we want to be

Over the past three decades, successive Governments have built up and refined the statutory framework for children with SEN. This strategy aims to personalise learning for all children, to make education more innovative and responsive to the diverse needs of individual children, so reducing our reliance on separate SEN structures and processes and raising the achievement of the many children – nearly one in six – who are considered to have SEN.

We have never been so well placed to deliver such a wide-ranging strategy to transform the lives and life chances of these children. The reform of children's services set out by *Every Child Matters*, with its focus on early intervention, preventative work, and integrated services for children through Children's Trusts, will deliver real and lasting benefits to children with SEN and their families. And our commitment to reducing child poverty, investing in early years education and childcare and targeting *support* at areas of social and economic deprivation will enable us to address the underlying causes of many children's difficulties in school.

2 *Excellence for all Children: Meeting Special Educational Needs* published by the Department for Education and Employment in 1997

3 *Meeting Special Educational Needs: A programme of Action* published by the Department for Education and Employment in 1998

4 *Special Educational Needs Code of Practice* (DfES/581/2001) published by the Department for Education and Skills in 2001 **wvvw.teachernet-gov.uk/sen**

5 *Special Educational Needs: a mainstream issue* published their Audit Commission in 2002 **www.audit-commission.gov.uk**

This strategy follows discussion with a wide range of practitioners and policy makers in schools, local authorities, the health service and the voluntary sector as well as children and young people. It sets out the Government's vision for the education of children with special educational needs and disabilities. It provides clear national leadership supported by an ambitious programme of sustained action and review, nationally and locally, over a number of years, in four key areas:

- **Early intervention** – to ensure that children who have difficulties learning receive the help they need as soon as possible and that parents of children with special educational needs and disabilities have access to suitable childcare (Chapter 1)
- **Removing barriers to learning** – by embedding inclusive practice in every school and early years setting (Chapter 2)
- **Raising expectations and achievement** – by developing teachers' skills and strategies for meeting the needs of children with SEN and sharpening our focus on the progress children make (Chapter 3)
- **Delivering improvements in partnership** – taking a hands-on approach to improvement so that parents can be confident that their child will get the education they need (Chapter 4).

We want all children, wherever they are educated, to have a good education that enables them to achieve to the full and provides a firm foundation for adult life. We want all pupils to have regular opportunities to learn, play and develop alongside each other, within their local community of schools, with shared responsibility and a partnership approach to their support.

We want parents to have confidence that their children's needs will be met effectively in school without feeling that the only way to achieve this is through a statement. In time, through action at local and national level to build the skills and capacity of schools to meet diverse pupil needs, we would expect only those children with the most severe and complex needs, requiring support from more than one specialist agency, to need the protection a statement provides.

We are committed to working in partnership to help all in the education service to deliver this vision, to unlock the potential of the many children who may have difficulty learning, but whose life chances depend on a good education.

What?

What does this tell you about the way the government have developed their strategy and their future plans for education?

This short section at the beginning of the SEN government strategy encapsulates many vital issues that will have a major influence on how pupils with SEN are supported and taught and on how services are delivered. As such it will clearly influence the way you will be asked to work in your educational setting. First it informs you that the government is committed to developing further the issues that appeared in the *National*

Curriculum Inclusion Statement (1999), *Inclusive schooling* (2001) and the *SEN Code of Practice* (2001). You are expected to be able to teach every child in your class whatever their level of need (with or without additional assistance) and to be able to provide them with an education that allows them to learn to the best of their ability. In this extract the government recognises that there is a need for further training and support for teachers if the SEN structures are going to be immersed in all classrooms and not be the responsibility of one or two specialists in the school. It also acknowledges that good practice may frequently mean integrated service support so that all aspects of a child's life is supported by many services, but under one umbrella; professionals working together with the child's needs at the centre of all discussions. Can this be achieved? You may say there isn't the time or the number of vital service professionals to enable this to happen, but the structures are being put in place to support the changes.

There is a commitment to explaining why the strategy wishes to rid the SEN system of the Statement of Educational Needs for all but those with the severest and most complex needs. This understanding is in line with the subsequent developments that reflect comments on the Statement of Special Educational Needs which is regarded as a perverse system that encourages teachers/other professionals to identify the deficits in a child and not focus on working with his/her strengths. It is also felt that Statements of Special Educational Need can act as exclusionary influences, perhaps enabling children to be unnecessarily separately educated from peers. This extract carefully and succinctly states ideas related to practice for deliberation and exploration. It also acknowledges that these changes set out are 'an ambitious programme' that will need *sustained action and review, nationally and locally, over a number of years* (DfES, 2004, Introduction).

Without a doubt this piece of legislation is further developing the inclusion agenda beyond that of purely education inclusion, building on the educational legislation and guidance previously issued. What else do you think needs to be developed to enable schools to move forwards with this agenda? Do you think it is based on educational research and monitoring and evaluation evidence?

Why?

Why was it necessary for the government to issue further legislation and guidance?

The government made it clear that it is not going to update or legalise the *SEN Code of Practice* (2001), but until the publication of *Removing barriers to achievement* (2004) it was unclear why, as many factors were beginning to influence the effectiveness of the system. This document clearly illustrated the evaluation and consultation work the government has done on the effectiveness of the current specialist approach to SEN.

Also in this era of global communication and easy access to information you can, as a practitioner, easily see if the Local Education Authority (LEA) you work for is responding to national legislation or not. National legislation should undoubtedly influence and guide local policies and hence individual school approaches. It provides data that you can evaluate or utilise for your individual needs and enables you to identify ways to alter unsatisfactory systems.

How?

How is the special educational needs legislation influencing the way the curriculum is taught in the classroom?

The monitoring and evaluation of the effectiveness of Individual Education Plans (IEPs) during the past couple of years is a good example of how legislation supports change. Since the *Warnock Report* (1978) and especially following the introduction and then the revision of the *SEN Code of Practice* (1994, 2001) IEPs have been written, usually termly, for pupils with special educational needs. Their effectiveness depends very much on how teachers use these documents; if used to help daily planning and preparation in the classroom they can be extremely efficient, but if once written they sit in the filing cabinet or in a file until it is time to review them then they are only a bureaucratic exercise and a waste of time. Clearly after consultation and evaluation the government has considered that especially for those pupils on the register for SEN at the School Action Level they are not efficient or effective for the pupils. However, the value of teachers planning, teaching and reflecting on the needs of every individual pupil is considered very beneficial as can be seen in this introductory section of *Removing barriers to achievement* (2004):

> This strategy aims to personalise learning for all children, to make education more innovative and responsive to the diverse needs of individual children, so reducing our reliance on separate SEN structures and processes (2004, Introduction).

This is just one example of how legislation can influence practice and vice versa and there are many more that can be identified within the curriculum focus of special educational needs.

Personal response

1. Do you feel, as a trainee teacher, that within the 'Where we want to be' section of *Removing barriers to achievement* (2004) the strategy aims are:
   - worthwhile;
   - significant;
   - important;
   - achievable?

If they are, why? If not, why not? Explain how you feel legislation influences practice using an actual example you have experienced.

2. How influential do you think SEN legislation has been in primary schools during the last 27 years?

Practical implications and activities

Take a detailed look at *one* of the areas listed below and see if you can trace its development during the last decade or so, using legislation to identify significant changes that influenced classroom practice:

- early intervention;
- removing barriers to learning;
- raising expectations and achievement;
- delivering improvements in partnership.

Focus as much as possible on the SEN legislation in all these areas. (Use the table below, or construct another similar one, to help you map legislation and then consider and reflect on the impact in the classroom for teachers and school communities.)

Example of chart to map development of SEN legislation and classroom practice

Early Intervention	Legislation	Impact
1.		
2.		

Further reading

Blandford, S (2005) *Remodelling schools*. London: Pearson.

Farrell, P (2001) 'Special education in the last twenty years: have things really got better?' *British Journal of Special Education* 28(1): 3–9.

Florian, L *et al.* (2004) 'What can national data sets tell us about inclusion and pupil achievement?' *British Journal of Special Education* vol.31(3): 115–121.

Gibson, S and Blandford, S (2005) *Managing special educational needs*. London: Paul Chapman.

Moore, J (1999) 'Developing a local authority response to inclusion'. *Support for learning* 14(4): 174–178.

Tassoni, P (2003) *Supporting special needs: understanding inclusion in the early years*. Oxford: Heinemann.

Thacker, J, Strudwick, D and Babbedge, E (2002) *Educating children with emotional and behavioural difficulties – inclusive practice in mainstream schools*. London: Routledge Falmer.

3 SEN policies in the primary phase

> **By the end of this chapter you should have considered and reflected upon:**
>
> - **why** policies for special educational needs are necessary within the primary phase in the twenty-first century;
> - **what** considerations and actions are necessary to be able to develop policies that demonstrate the changing role of 'special educational needs' within the inclusion agenda;
> - **how** SEN policies reflect the ethos of a school.
>
> **Linking your learning**
> *Achieving QTS: Professional studies primary phase*, second edition, Jacques, K and Hyland, R (2003) Chapter 12.
>
> **Professional Standards for QTS**
> 2.6, 3.1.1, 3.3.2, 3.3.3, 3.3.4

Introduction

Special educational needs policies need to be considered at various levels – government, local and individual schools. Since the introduction of the *Special Educational Needs Code of Practice* (DfEE, 1994) the management of 'SEN policy' for Local Education Authorities and every school has been regulated by legislation. Although not a statutory requirement in itself, every school had to and still has to pay regard to the *SEN Code of Practice* (1994 and 2001). Some regulations, such as those involving Statements of Educational Needs are also legally binding. Other published documents also influence SEN policy within schools on a daily basis. These are:

Government level

- *Circular 6/94 (Part 1)* (DfEE, 1994)
- *Excellence for all children* (DEE, 1997)
- *National Standards for Special Educational Needs co-ordinators* (TTA, 1998)
- *National Special Educational Needs Specialist Standards* (TTA, 1999)
- *The National Curriculum Inclusion Statement* (QCA, 1999, 458)
- *Inclusive schooling: children with special educational needs* (DfES, 2001a)
- *Special Educational Needs Code of Practice* (DfES, 2001b)
- *SEN toolkit, section 1: principles and policies* (DfES, 2001c)

Local level

The *Special Educational Needs Code of Practice* (DfES, 2001b) states that Local Education Authorities' (LEAs) (soon to be named Local Authorities (LAs)) SEN policies must include how to:

- promote high standards, inclusion and equal opportunities;
- collaborate with early education settings, schools and other services and agencies;
- develop partnerships with parents;
- encourage the participation of children and young people with SEN in making decisions about their education.

Within this LEA policy framework there is also the requirement to:

- review and update the policy and development plans on a regular basis;
- develop their SEN policies in consultation with schools and their other partners and keep them under review.

Individual school level

At an individual school level the *SEN Code of Practice* (2001) again enforces that:

- schools *must* have a written SEN policy;
- the SEN policy *must* contain the information as set out in the Education (Special Educational Needs) Information England Regulations 1999 at Annex A;
- governing bodies of all maintained mainstream schools must publish information about, and report on, the school's policy on special educational needs . . . While the governing body and the head teacher will take overall responsibility for the school's SEN policy, the school as a whole should be involved in its development;
- as with all policies, the SEN policy should be subject to a regular cycle of monitoring, evaluation and review. Thus governing bodies *must* on at least an annual basis, consider and report on the effectiveness of the school's work on behalf of children with special educational needs;
- the governing body's annual report *must* include information on the implementation of the governing body's policy on pupils with special educational needs and any changes to the policy during the last year;
- all members of staff have important responsibilities. In practice the division of day-to-day responsibilities is a matter for individual schools, to be decided in the light of a school's circumstances and size, priorities and ethos;
- all teaching and non-teaching staff should be involved in the development of the school's SEN policy (DfES, 2001b, 1:23–1:39, 12–15).

As a practitioner you will need to know the LEA SEN policy as well as your own school's SEN policy. The latter of these should inform you about how the school in which you are working regards:

- children with SEN;
- inclusive practice;
- the learning needs of *all* children.

The SENCO or SEN team will support the policy on a daily basis, but in the classroom you, the teacher, are responsible for *all* the educational needs of *all* the children within your care.

Before you read the following extract, prepare yourself by reading:

- Armstrong, F (1998) 'Curricula, "management" and special and inclusive education', in Clough, P (ed) *Managing inclusive education – from policy to experience*, London: Paul Chapman.
- Constable, D (2002) *Planning and organising the SENCO Year, pp11–30*. London: David Fulton.
- DfES, (2001b) *Special Educational Needs Code of Practice*, Chapter 1, 1:13–1:39, pp9–15. Annesley: DfES.
- Gibson, S and Blandford, S (2005) *Managing Special Educational Needs*, London: Paul Chapman.
- TTA (1998), *The national standards for special educational needs co-ordinators*, London: TTA.

Extract: Farrell, M. (2001) *Standards and special educational needs*, **pp75–76, London: Continuum.**

Teaching Pupils with SEN

Related to this are developments in setting standards for SEN coordinators (Teacher Training Agency, 1998b, 2000) and specialist standards (Teacher Training Agency, 1999).

The *National Standards for Special Educational Needs Co-ordinators* (Teacher Training Agency, 1998b) sets out the core purpose of the SEN coordinator (SENCO), the key outcomes of SEN coordination, professional knowledge and understanding, skills and attributes, and key areas of SEN coordination. In many parts of the document there are less precise references to meeting needs, with no indication of what this would mean or how it would be known if needs were met. Elsewhere, however, there are more purposeful references to standards and access.

Among the key outcomes for SEN coordination are that pupils on the SEN register 'show improvement in literacy, numeracy and information technology skills' and that such pupils are 'helped to access the curriculum'. While teachers should be familiar with and implement 'approaches to meeting the needs of pupils with SEN', learning support assistants should become knowledgeable in 'ways of supporting pupils and help them to maximise their levels of achievement and independence' (p6).

In professional knowledge and understanding, the SENCO should have knowledge and understanding of, among many other things, 'the main strategies for improving and sustaining high standards of pupil achievement' and (in collaboration with the information technology coordinator), how IT 'can be used to help pupils gain access to the curriculum' (p8).

Key areas of SEN coordination include that SENCOs 'support staff in understanding the learning needs of pupils with SEN and the importance of raising their achievement' (p12). SENCOs also should 'support the development of improvement in literacy, numeracy and information technology skills, as well as access to the wider curriculum' (p13).

To take another example, in the *National Special Educational Needs Specialist Standards* (Teacher Training Agency, 1999) the core standards refer to the development of literacy, numeracy and information and communication technology (ICT). The skills and attributes required of teachers working with pupils with severe or complex SEN indicate the importance of raising standards of pupil achievement.

The same principles of good teaching apply to all pupils, including those with SEN, and it is therefore reasonable to judge teaching according to the progress of pupils with SEN. It may be that such pupils start from a lower starting point than the average in, say, reading or mathematics, but the progress and the subsequent standards reached can be used as an indication of teaching quality.

In assessments of the quality of teaching, the contribution of learning support assistants is often an important factor. The work of the teacher (who assumes overall responsibility for the learning of pupils) with the learning support assistant can be judged according to the extent to which it improves standards of pupil achievement. Factors such as clear shared learning objectives, shared planning and monitoring by the teacher of what the pupils with SEN have learnt are important.

Why?

Why maintain *The National Standards for Special Educational Needs Co-ordinators* (TTA, 1998) and the role of the SENCO if 'the same principles of good teaching apply to all pupils' (Farrell, 2001, p76)?

As a classroom teacher you may suggest that the consideration of this extract is not of personal interest. However, beyond the core purpose of the SENCO, the key areas and outcomes of SEN co-ordination and the *professional knowledge and understanding, skills and attributes* (Farrell, 2001, p75) there are statements that are very relevant for every teacher. Also since 1998 the role and responsibilities of the SENCO have changed in many schools to complement the developing inclusion agenda.

The core purpose remains the same in essence, but the practical aspects of the role are altering in line with developing teacher expertise and individual children's needs. SENCOs have during the last decade been the conduits of knowledge and support in the field of SEN, helping individual pupils with SEN and staff in mainstream environments adjust to the changes demanded, first from integration and now inclusion policies. Bureaucracy and workload pressures undoubtedly have also influenced the rethinking of the responsibilities of a SENCO. Is this role becoming a 'dinosaur', outstaying its usefulness, or is it going to survive as long as inclusive practice fails to be fully implemented?

What?

What influence do SEN policies have on standards and achievement?

Your experience as a practitioner will have illustrated to you already that schools are all at different stages of development with different needs and main focuses of improvement. Policy actually means intended action and it is considered that if supported by senior managers, SEN (and the SENCO) may function as a 'catalyst for change' (Cowne, 1998, p12). Current literature (Cowne, 1998; Corbett, 2001; Lindsay, 2003) and government guidance (DfES, 2001b; DfES, 2004; DfES, 2004a) emphasise that if effective in practice, as well as in policy, the SEN policy will result in the improvement and achievement of all pupils. Why? If policy is realistic, but thorough and child-centred at an individual level, it will stress the importance of early identification, good record keeping (monitoring and assessment), active partnerships between school and parents and organise the appropriate use of support. Reflect on why all policies in a school should/but do not have a similar approach to learning. With the introduction of personalised learning for all children with its five core elements (published in September 2004) and listed below, the role of SEN policies may alter.

1. Assessment for learning.
2. Teaching and learning strategies.
3. Curriculum entitlement and choice.
4. A student centred approach to school organisation.
5. Strong partnership beyond the school (ESRC, 2004).

This factor is again illustrated in further guidance (DfES, 2004a, p2):

> The materials do not therefore concentrate on approaches for children with specific labels or disabilities. They focus on the conditions that will enhance the learning of all children, including those children with severe and/or complex SEN. They attempt to make overt some of the intuitive and additional practices demonstrated by confident and experienced teachers that help children who have difficulties to learn more effectively.

How?

How important therefore are SEN policies to me as a classroom practitioner?

You will need to ask yourself how important it is to you to understand the ethos and circumstances of the school in which you are working? How important is it to access whole school systems to support you in the teaching of every individual child in your class? Currently SEN policies should incorporate many aspects of a school's intentions to move forward with inclusion and the government 'social agenda' (HMSO, 2003) including personalised learning and lifelong learning. It will include information about the legislation that remains to ensure children with SEN are provided for appropriately and with the best possible resources and teaching available to that individual school. It may for example start with a paragraph such as:

> *All children have skills, talents and abilities and as a school we have a responsibility to develop these to the full.* (Constable, 2002, p17)

From these illustrations you can see how you can identify the importance a school places on the change agenda and the individual needs of every pupil in its community through its SEN policy, which annually goes through a reviewing process involving all staff members and the governing body.

Personal response

1. Critically consider the role you feel SEN policies have played in effecting change in practice during the last decade. Use the literature and guidance listed above to enhance your understanding of the evolving process of change that has taken place.

2. Now reflect on whether you believe SEN policies will play such an influential role during the forthcoming decade as it did in the last. Evaluate carefully what information you are utilising to arrive at your conclusions – is it based on sound evidence, conjecture or governmental or personal opinion?

Practical implications and activities

1. Critically examine with colleagues the phrase 'good teaching is good teaching for all' (DfES, 2004b). Explore through your reading or experience to date whether you feel there is a specific SEN pedagogy or not.

2. What do you think about the following suggestions from the DfES of good classroom practice, arising from the National Inclusion Statement principles (DfES, 2000)?

Children will be more effectively included where appropriate consideration has been given to:

- what the child will learn;
- what teaching methods will be used;
- what ways of bypassing barriers to learning have been chosen for particular children. (DfES, 2004a, p3)

Carefully scrutinise how different these are to the requirements set out in the *Special Educational Needs Code of Practice* (2001) in which interventions and systems such as Individual Education Plans (ICPs) were incorporated.

If they do not differ totally, what in your opinion is the 'change' factor being sought? Will it involve or be led by SEN policy or not ?

Further consider how this is being implemented by the government and who they are involving, asking to lead, the change?

Further reading

Constable, D (2002) *Planning and organising the SENCO year*. London: David Fulton.

Corbett, J (2001) Teaching approaches which support inclusive education: a connective pedagogy. *British Journal of Special Education*, 28(2): 55–59.

Cowne, E (1998) *The SENCO handbook* (2nd edn). London: David Fulton.

DfES (2001b) *Special Educational Needs Code of Practice*. Annesley: DfES.

DfES (2004) *Removing barriers to achievement*. Annesley: DfES.

DfES (2004a) *Primary National Strategy, learning and teaching for children with special educational needs in the primary years*. Annesley: DfES.

DfES (2004b) *Teaching strategies and approaches for pupils with special educational needs*. Research Report RR516.

Economic and Social Research Council (2004) *Personalised learning*. ESRC.

HMSO (2003) *Every child matters*. Norwich: The Stationery Office.

Lindsay, G. (2003) Inclusive education: a critical perspective. *British Journal of Special Education*. 30(1): 3–12.

QCA (1999) *The National Curriculum Inclusion Statement*, 458. Sudbury: QCA.

Teacher Training Agency (1998) *National Standards for Special Educational Needs Co-ordinators*. London: TTA.

Teacher Training Agency (1999) *National Special Educational Needs Specialist Standards*. London: TTA.

Extract: Rose, R and Howley, M (2001) Chapter 5 'Entitlement or denial? The curriculum and its influence upon inclusion processes', in O'Brien, T (ed) *Enabling inclusion, blue skies . . . dark clouds*. London: Optimus Publishing. Read 'The shape of the future needs provision'.

The shape of future needs provision

If we are to raise educational standards by addressing the needs of all pupils, we will need to draw upon the experience of all teachers. This must include those working in special schools and other forms of special provision who have committed themselves to working with those pupils who have traditionally been excluded from the mainstream. Many of these teachers have skills and understanding which have been critical in the development of teaching approaches and which have found favour with a significant number of parents who choose to send their children to a special school. To concentrate our attention solely upon the changes necessary in mainstream schools – while ignoring the significant advances in teaching pupils with special needs which have been made in special schools – is more likely to alienate policy-makers and advocates of full inclusion from those who have worked closely with the very pupils for whom inclusion is seen as providing the greatest benefit. In order to make progress in addressing this most complex of issues, it is necessary to draw upon all the experience and expertise available. This will include both teachers in mainstream and special schools. We should also be mindful of those teachers who through their work in specialist provision, often with pupils who have well-defined and specific needs such as autism or sensory impairments, have developed an understanding of how both integrated and segregated arrangements work. It may be that some of these colleagues can provide insights into the pragmatics of educating pupils in a variety of settings that other teachers do not have.

The Green Paper *Excellence for All Children* (DfEE, 1997) suggests that future provision for pupils with SEN will need to be developed along a continuum which includes the retention of some special schools. Such an assertion may be interpreted as recognition that there are some pupils for whom a mainstream placement may not be a realistic goal. However, in accepting that for the majority of pupils a mainstream education will be the model of future provision, there is a danger that if special schools do not change, they will become isolated, and for some pupils the opportunities for contact with their mainstream peers will be lost. Special schools will need to establish close links with the mainstream which have a clearly defined and mutually beneficial basis. While much of the enthusiasm for, and experience of, working with pupils who have the most complex needs has been retained within special schools, few mainstream schools have benefited from or had access to this expertise. In order to promote inclusion based upon learning processes, rather than upon location, there is a need to develop an education system which provides greater ease of transition between phases, and mutual support. This has been recognised in the Green Paper (DfEE, 1997) suggesting that teachers in special schools should provide specialist support for their colleagues in the mainstream. Such a proposal needs to be further developed, with the establishment of formal agreements, that build upon the *ad hoc* approach to co-operation which currently exists.

If future models of provision are based upon a continuum, there must be recognition that for some pupils transition from special to mainstream school, and vice versa, will become the norm. Schools will have a responsibility to ensure that such transitions can take place without adding further to the difficulties faced by the pupils concerned. Suggestions have been made (Jenkinson, 1997) that for some pupils a placement in two settings may be appropriate. This requires the establishment of cross-phase consistent procedures and also a requirement that schools examine their curriculum to ensure that all pupils have their individual needs recognised, providing content, teaching approaches, and resources to address these. Such a model will not be achieved without changes to the curriculum and its management. There must be a demand that the curriculum on offer in the special school, while complementing, and to a large extent overlapping that available in the mainstream, provides those 'specialist' elements which justify provision which is separate. If pupils are to be defined in terms of their curriculum needs, and these do not differ from those of their mainstream peers, there is no justification for education within a special school. Special schools must demonstrate that through a careful analysis of the needs of the individual they can tailor a curriculum which meets those needs which are unique to the individual, while recognising the rights of the pupil to be given access to mainstream peers.

This analysis extends beyond a simplistic assessment of pupil abilities. Logan and Malone (1998), in examining pupil reactions and participation in a range of instructional contexts, recognise that for many pupils with SEN alterations will need to be made to the traditional delivery modes encountered in mainstream classes. The practicalities of achieving such change will inevitably prove challenging to all schools and may be impossible for some. Adjusting the curriculum to meet the needs of all pupils will demand an increased flexibility in terms of placement arrangements. Special and mainstream schools working in tandem may be the only way of achieving such a supportive learning system.

Why?

Why do SEN policies need to recognise the significant role special schools will play in developing inclusive practices further?

The issue of special schooling within the inclusion agenda is one that creates strong reactions and one which I suspect you also have very firm feelings about. However, for this section of the chapter I do not want to focus on whether there should be specialist provision in all Local Education Authorities for pupils, as a general line of discussion. Within the development of SEN policies there are a group of teachers whose skills need to be utilised fully for the benefit of all children. Recent years have seen significant advances in teaching children with special educational needs within special schools. Rose and Howley (2001) suggested that these professionals have knowledge and experience of both sectors and can therefore practically support the changing face of SEN policy. Recent government legislation (DfES, 2004, pp38–39) has also recognised the need to *promote collaboration between special and mainstream schools to support school improvement* to *make the most of their skills and expertise, and to offer inclusive experiences for all pupils, working in partnership with the local authority.* SEN policies have therefore altered to recognise that:

- special school staff need to be equal partners in SEN policy;
- active collaboration is beneficial for all school adults and children;
- specialist provision can provide outreach and tailored packages of support for children, for example, with 'low incidence needs' or social, emotional and behavioural needs (SEBN).

In acknowledging these skills and needs legislation and guidance is continuing along the inclusive agenda, but in a way that is supportive of current learners and adults who need time and opportunities to make mindset changes to their practices.

How?

How can there be the acceptance of collaboration with special schools within mainstream schools' SEN policies?

Your understanding of what inclusive practice is will determine the way in which you consider this question. However, government guidance *Removing barriers to achievement* (DfES, 2004) in its introduction indicates clearly the present expectations of schools: *all teachers should expect to teach children with special educational needs*

(SEN) and all schools should play their part in educating children from their local community, whatever their background or ability. The need to reduce, not get rid of, reliance on separate SEN structures and processes, as well as raising the achievement of children with SEN is also stated early on within this document (DfES 2004, Introduction). Therefore, despite theoretical debates about whether there is a special needs pedagogy or not (Norwich and Lewis, 2005), the government states quite clearly that: *including all in their local communities, and raising the achievement of children with special educational needs* are its main concerns. In many ways this illustrates that as long as a special school is part of a group of local schools collaborating and using flexible packages of outreach and support for all children, a positive role can be played in the development of SEN policy and the inclusion agenda.

What?

What does this mean for you?

The word 'flexibility' is vital throughout this debate. If schools collaborate as 'clusters' drawing on the expertise and knowledge of all staff to support one another, I can only make an assumption that as long as time and opportunities are made available for all staff to access this, you as a new practitioner will have additional support and guidance easily available to you on a regular basis. In time, this flexibility of use of skills and expertise should provide you with practical skills you would have only been able to previously learn about, via training outside of your workplace setting. Does this therefore actually enable the establishment of greater inclusive practices throughout all schools without additional resources from outside the local community of schools?

Personal response

The issue of SEN policies at face value looks extremely straightforward and non-controversial. In fact, as has been seen, it is a complex issue with many facets and implications.

How would you like to see SEN policy developing within the next five years? Indeed do you think there is a need for separate SEN policies at all within this current inclusive environment?

What will influence, in your opinion, the direction it will take?

To help you formulate your thoughts and ideas in a critical manner draw a mind map illustrating all the areas of school life and curricula on which special educational needs has an influence. Is there a better way to look at individual children's learning and social needs?

Practical implications and activities

1. Create a list of all the policies you can think of that are readily available within the mainstream schools you have taught in. How many of them actually mention issues of learning and teaching that would affect children with special educational needs?

2. Is there still a requirement to have a separate SEN policy? Critically evaluate your answers with a colleague, and also if the opportunity is available speak to a parent of a child who either has a Statement of Educational Needs or receives – School Action Plus input. How do their responses alter or adapt your thoughts, if at all? To help you with this activity use the Circular 6/94 (DfEE, 1994) and the Special Educational Needs Code of Practice (DfES, 2001b).

3. Finally do you feel there is still the need for a SENCO or SEN teacher within the developing framework of collaborative and inclusive schooling? Explore the roles and responsibilities of a SENCO and see who would fulfil these core purposes (if indeed you feel they are still required) if the SEN system was felt irreconcilable with the developing agendas. Use the specialist standards to help you with this task (TTA, 1998).

Further reading

Constable, D (2002) *Planning and organising the SENCO Year*. London: David Fulton.

DfEE (1994) *The organisation of special educational provision. Circular 6.94*, Annesley: DfEE.

DfES (2001b) *Special Educational Needs Code of Practice*. Annesley: DfES.

DfES (2004) *Removing barriers to achievement*. Annesley: DfES.

Norwich, B and Lewis, A (2005) 'How specialized is teaching pupils with disabilities and difficulties?', in Lewis, A and Norwich, B (eds) *Special teaching for special children? – pedagogies for inclusion*. Maidenhead: OUP.

Teacher Training Agency (1998) *National Standards for Special Educational Needs Co-ordinators*. London: TTA.

Teacher Training Agency (1999) *National Special Educational Needs Specialist Standards*. London: TTA.

4 SEN and inclusion

> **By the end of this chapter you should have considered and reflected upon:**
>
> - **why** it is necessary to maintain active debate about special educational needs and inclusion;
> - **what** principles and policies have influenced the direction of SEN within the wider agendas of educational and social inclusion;
> - **how** special educational needs will continue to be an important aspect of practical daily life in a primary school.
>
> **Linking your learning**
> *Achieving QTS: Professional studies primary phase*, second edition, Jacques, K and Hyland, R (2003) Chapter 12.
>
> **Professional Standards for QTS**
> 1.1, 1.2, 1.3, 2.4, 2.6, 2.7, 3.1.1, 3.1.2, 3.1.3, 3.2.4, 3.2.5, 3.2.6, 3.3.1, 3.3.4, 3.3.5, 3.3.6, 3.3.14

Introduction

The identification of the relevant Qualified Teacher Status references for this chapter was challenging, not because of what to put in, but what to leave out. I hope you can see the main areas of importance I have eventually decided to focus on.

The term 'inclusion' still has a variety of meanings for different people. Teachers, support staff, parents, LEA staff, government officials and even children are all working along this 'inclusive practice' path supposedly together. In reality, however, it must be acknowledged, that they are not in many cases walking at the same speed or even in the exact same direction, due to:

- very different experiential and theoretical backgrounds;
- diverse personally-held views of inclusion, influenced by feelings about how it will effect them, their roles or their children.

Being a process and not a fixed state like integration, inclusive practice is difficult to quantify, but it is generally agreed that *inclusion is an active, not a passive process* (Corbett, 2001, p55). Therefore change is to be expected and over the last few years, led by government guidance and legislation, the boundaries of inclusion for practitioners within schools have extended still further. You can see this by looking at how *The Special Educational Needs Code of Practice* (DfES,2001b), then *Inclusive schooling* (DfES, 2001a) and the *Index of inclusion* (Booth and Ainsow, 2002) and significantly *Every child matters* (HMSO, 2003) and *Removing barriers to achievement* (DfES,

2004) all define inclusion. I will ask you to return to this issue further on in this chapter. Succinctly, the meaning of inclusion has radiated from:

- including children with special educational needs in mainstream schools, (DfES, 2001);

  to

- *inclusion is about the education of all children and young people* (CSIE, 2002, p1); *inclusion in education is just one aspect of inclusion in society* (Soan, 2004, p9);

  and to date to:

- educational and social inclusion with five key outcomes:
  1. Being healthy.
  2. Staying safe.
  3. Enjoying and achieving.
  4. Making a positive contribution.
  5. Economic well-being. (HMSO, 2003, p14)

It is therefore not surprising that it is taking a considerable amount of time to build partnerships and systems that can be developed in line with an ever changing agenda, led by government legislation, but with limited debate or reflection on how this will impact on the practitioners and children on the ground level. Pupils with special educational needs are thus only part of the new broader inclusion agenda, but they are a significant part whose needs are still protected by legislation and will undoubtedly continue to influence developments.

The two extracts provided for you within this chapter consider the inclusion debate as it stood leading up to 2001. Much has changed since then and practices in schools have significantly altered for many, which you will need to bear in mind, but they do provide extremely clear views of inclusion at that time, giving you a very good foundation on which to explore and critically evaluate current polices and principles.

Before you read the following extract, prepare yourself by reading:

- Corbett, J (2001), 'Teaching approaches which support inclusive education: a connective pedagogy'. *British Journal of Special Education*; 28(2): 55–59.
- DfES, (2001a) *Inclusive schooling: children with special educational needs*, pp1–3. Annesley: DfES.
- DfES (2001b) *Special Educational Needs Code of Practice*, p7. Annesley: DfES.
- DfES, (2004) *Removing barriers to achievement*. Annesley: DfES.
- HMSO, (2003) *Every child matters*. Norwich: The Stationery Office.
- Jarvis, J, Iantaffi, A and Sinka, I (2003) 'Inclusion in mainstream classrooms: experiences of deaf pupils', pp206–218, in Nind *et al.*, *Inclusive education: diverse perspectives*. London: David Fulton.
- Soan, S (2004) 'Recent legislation, AEN and inclusion', pp8–12., in Soan, S (ed) *Additional educational needs – inclusive approaches to teaching*. London: David Fulton.

Extract: Dyson, A (2001) 'Special needs in the twenty-first century: where we've been and where we're going'. *British Journal of Special Education* **28(1): 27–28. Read section: 'Coming to terms with the future'.**

Coming to terms with the future

It is my contention that the inherent instability of the present means that it is incumbent on us to look carefully at what the future might hold. Even as the 'new' resolution of 'inclusion' struggles to establish its hegemony, we should, I believe, try to understand how it will ultimately fragment and what possibilities might open up for alternative resolutions. Moreover, despite the apparent conservatism of the 'inclusion backlash', there are indications that those possibilities might consist of more than a return to the *status quo ante*. One such possibility is the emergence of the *social* inclusion agenda.

In the 1997 SEN Green Paper (DfEE, 1997), DfEE used the term 'inclusion', it seemed, to refer to an extension of the process of integration that had been under way for well over two decades. Since then, however, the Government and, in particular, David Blunkett have tended to elide inclusion in this sense with the notion of '*social* inclusion' (Blunkett, 1999a; 1999b; 2000). This latter term seems to mean something that is allied to, but not quite synonymous with the former. Blunkett's 1999(a) CBI speech, for instance, describes a 'drive for inclusion' in the following terms:

> 'Our Green Paper on special educational needs has resulted in almost £60m being made available to support SEN pupils and improve access to buildings; LEAs now have targets to reduce truancy and exclusions by a third, and the New Deal for 18–24 year olds is ensuring that all those who have left school without the necessary skills are in work or training with charitable or voluntary organisations or employers, and have advice tailored to their needs.'

What is significant here is the way that the notion of inclusion slips from a classic concern with access for 'SEN pupils' to a new discourse which is to do with truancy, (disciplinary) exclusion, and progression to work and training. What a more extended reading of Blunkett's speeches reveals, in fact, is that *social* inclusion is concerned with far more than where children with special educational needs receive their education. Rather, social inclusion – a key concept in the 'third way' ideology (Giddens, 1998) is about building a cohesive society, by ensuring that no social groups become alienated from the mainstream. This in turn means equipping potentially marginalised groups with the capacity to become active citizens and, crucially, with the skills they will need to survive in an increasingly competitive and skills-hungry job market. The social inclusion agenda, therefore, is linked to the wider standards agenda through which the Government ultimately seeks to create a highly skilled workforce capable of maintaining a high-tech economy. As Blunkett (1999b) puts it elsewhere:

> 'Finding a way of giving people a stake will be critical. The Thatcher era attempted to do this through shareholding but succeeded in excluding those with few material resources. Our approach must be more inclusive and it must be two-way. We need to recognise that for most people – particularly those who are

disadvantaged materially – personal initiative, skills and the ability to capitalise on labour market opportunities are now the keys to success and to having a tangible stake in society. Skills and human capital are the new forms of wealth and security in which people can share.'

Not surprisingly, this new agenda has generated a wide range of initiatives which embrace, but also go well beyond issues in special needs education. Some of these – Sure Start (DfEE, 1999c), say, or the Connexions Service (DfEE, 2000) are neutral, or even supportive, of the inclusion agenda *per se*. Others, however – Excellence in Cities (DfEE, 1999a), with its 'learning support units', Education Action Zones (DfEE, 1999b), with their overwhelming emphasis on targets for raised attainment, or the study support programme, with its overtones of remedial education – seem, at best, little concerned with the placement of children with special educational needs and may, at worst, be positively inimical to some of the principles of participation embodied in, say, the *Index for Inclusion* (Booth et al, 2000). In crude terms, whilst the *inclusion* agenda focuses on presence and participation, *social* inclusion focuses much more on educational outcomes and, particularly, on the re-engagement of marginalised groups with learning, whether or not that engagement takes place in the context of the 'common' classroom, school and curriculum.

We can already see examples of schools which are *socially* inclusive in the Government's sense, but whose commitment to inclusion *per se* is ambiguous, to say the least. Elsewhere (Dyson & Millward, 2000), Alan Millward and I have described schools serving areas of social disadvantage which have sought to drive up 'standards' amongst their lowest attainers and to engage their most disaffected students in education not through a commitment to participation in shared learning experiences with their peers, but through alternative curriculum and provision – perhaps outside school – an unrelenting focus on 'basic skills', a policy of (virtually) zero tolerance towards disruptive behaviour and so on. Similarly, our current collaborative research with schools on how they can develop their responses to the inclusion agenda is finding that their concerns are not primarily about the presence and participation of students 'with special educational needs'; they are about issues in social inclusion – changing cultural attitudes to schooling in areas of social disadvantage, for instance, or finding ways of reducing truancy, or improving the writing skills of boys.

What this social inclusion agenda, both at Government and at school level, offers us, is an emerging alternative resolution of what we earlier called the 'dilemma of difference'. This resolution pays attention to other aspects of difference than those which concern inclusion *per se*. Its focus is on marginalisation, alienation and exclusion from employment – not on special needs or on disability as such. It offers a different view of what it means to be 'included' – a view which is about acquiring essential skills, surviving in a competitive labour market and active engagement with a stakeholder democracy rather than about participating as an equally valued member of a common social institution. And it proposes different means of realising its ideals – not individual programming and cultural change within institutions, but intensive training and support, frequently targeted on areas and groups rather than on individuals, in order to ensure that everyone has at least some minimum level of skills and resources to enable them to survive in a competitive environment. Given the capacity which Government has to exert pressure on the education system, it seems probable that it is this version of inclusion that will come to dominate the future – at least in the medium term. Whether inclusion as it is understood within the special needs field will be subsumed within this wider agenda, or will simply disappear in the face of it, is something which remains to be seen.

References

Ainscow, M (1999) *Understanding the Development of Inclusive Schools*. London: Falmer Press.

Ainscow, M (2000) 'The next step for special education: supporting the development of inclusive practices', *British Journal of Special Education*. 27 (2), 76–80.

Artiles, A J (1998) 'The dilemma of difference: enriching the disproportionality discourse with theory and context', *The Journal of Special Education*. 32 (1), pp32–36.

Bines, H (1986) *Redefining Remedial Education*. Beckenham: Croom Helm.

Why?

Why is special educational needs still very much part of the inclusion agenda?

> Whether inclusion as it is understood within the special needs field will be subsumed within this wider agenda, or simply disappear in the face of it, is something which remains to be seen.
>
> (Dyson, 2001, p28)

Educational and social inclusion policies and principles both value and celebrate difference. With this in mind it is easy to see that identifying and supporting learners with special educational needs will still remain a focus of importance for schools. However SEN is no longer viewed as the deficit medical model of the 1980s and most of the 1990s, where the difficulty was the child's difficulty and he / she had to adapt to the teacher's methods and school environment. Also the inclusion debate, as Hanko (2003, p125) explains: *is no longer concerned merely with the extent to which mainstream schools are able to accommodate all children regardless of need, but increasingly focuses on institutional improvement in understanding the range of their needs.*

Schools are examining their systems and ethos, teachers are being supported and trained to teach in a manner that enables pupils, through differentiation and an awareness of learning and environmental preferences, to be active and motivated learners. SENCOs and SEN staff in mainstream and special schools, with their expertise and experience in teaching and learning with children with complex, or severe behavioural and emotional needs, therefore become vital resources in facilitating this change of focus, in many cases becoming the supporters and trainers of teachers and support staff within their community/cluster of schools. Rather than disappearing therefore special educational needs is being utilised as a tool to enhance the learning of all pupils, by using and adapting practices usually reserved for the 'remedial/special needs groups' within mainstream classrooms.

How?

How will inclusion further enhance special educational needs?

During the 1980s and up until the end of the 1990s special educational needs very much followed a deficit medical model of support whereby the difficulty was the child's problem. In this environment the child had to adapt (integration) to the curriculum and the school systems, and if he or she could not achieve this then they would be required to attend a special school. Children on the special needs register of a mainstream school were 'the responsibility of the SENCO' and the teacher did not have to try to adapt his/her teaching or strategies to try to help pupils learn within the whole class situation. This not only meant that frequently learning was limited, but socially children were not accepted by others in their own class. That was why when a child misbehaved or became a problem the class teacher always sent for the SENCO. Teachers were not expected to expand their skills and understanding by planning and working with pupils with special educational needs and so the SENCO and SEN team quickly became the 'experts' in SEN.

With the introduction of inclusive education, the implementation of the revised *Special Educational Needs Code of Practice* (DfES, 2001b) and other important guidance and legislation such as the *Index for inclusion* (Booth and Ainscow, 2002) the medical model was no longer a responsible method of supporting learners with additional and special needs. Accommodating pupils, whatever their need, was also not ensuring their engagement and participation in the curriculum and social life of the community. As Hanko (2003, p. 125) said: *The inclusion debate ... increasingly focuses on institutional improvement in understanding the range of their (children's) needs.*

The SEN strategy *Removing barriers to achievement* (DfES, 2004, Introduction) states:

> All teachers should expect to teach children with special educational needs (SEN) and all schools should play their part in educating children from their local community, whatever their background or ability.

This means that all teachers are now required to have the knowledge and skills to teach all children with special educational needs, with guidance and support from more experienced teachers, SENCOs and special school staff. Schools have to ensure they have adapted their curriculum, teaching methods and used appropriate resources to enable all children the opportunity to learn as much as they can, in a way that encourages independence, good self-esteem and positive social skills. If achieved, inclusion can not be seen as a negative initiative/change for children with special educational needs, but a positive opportunity that allows flexibility within a system so that their needs can be met in the most appropriate way for each individual.

What?

What are the necessary skills and knowledge a classroom practitioner requires to work with children with SEN, within an inclusive primary school community?

You will need to work in a client-centred manner that will enable you to:

- help pupils understand how they learn (metacognition);
- separate any disabilities from the persona;
- recognise each pupil's needs and strengths;
- work together from shared knowledge and understanding of the way individual pupils learn. (Horsfall, 2004)

You will have an important role to play in fostering well founded understanding of inclusive practice and thinking within the whole community and this can be achieved by engaging proactively with all other members of the school (Gibson and Blandford, 2005). Allan (2003, p.178) argues that it is important to: *listen to what children and their parents say about what inclusion means to them; and recognising the way in which we ourselves are implicated in practices that exclude.*

Also undoubtedly you will need support and additional training to meet all the individual challenges you may experience, but most importantly you will need to have a willingness to explore, to be adaptable and to enjoy *all* the children within your class whatever their difference or need.

Personal response

Do you consider that with the publication of *Every child matters* (HMSO, 2003) and *Removing barriers to achievement* (DfES, 2004) inclusive practice has begun to focus on the rights of children and the effectiveness of their education? Discuss with a colleague, before reflecting on the following quotation and question.

Lindsay (2003,p10) writes:

There is a need to develop beyond concerns about inputs and settings to a focus on experiences and outcomes and to attempt to identify causal relationships.

Read and critically examine this statement. Do you agree with this? Are schools focusing on experiences and outcomes as yet?

Practical implications and activities

1. Examine in a critical manner with a colleague the following three statements given by pupils with either profound or moderate hearing loss. Using your understanding and knowledge of what educational inclusion is, as well as literature and policy documentation, formulate an argument illustrating how inclusive you feel these examples demonstrate the learning environments within these schools are.

Statements

It is good that it is mixed here, you can have more friends. Deaf pupils can teach hearing to sign and hearing pupils can teach deaf to speak. It will help for the future when you work with hearing or go out with hearing friends.

I prefer teachers here, at the Unit, than the mainstream teachers. Here they help me to understand the meaning. The mainstream teachers don't, they talk too fast.

With a group of hearing people talking I feel left out. One girl signs for me but the others wouldn't wait and carry on talking. They say I talk like a baby

(Nind *et al.*, 2003, pp211–215).

2. What do you think the schools in question need to explore in relation to their ethos and ability to engender an inclusive environment for their pupils with special educational needs? Consider critically.

Further reading

Gibson, S and Blandford, S (2005) *Managing special educational needs*. London: Paul Chapman.

Horsfall, B (2004) 'Special educational needs and the teacher', in Jacques, K and Hyland, R *Achieving QTS, Professional studies – primary phase*. Exeter: Learning Matters.

Jones, P (2005) 'Inclusion: lessons from the children'. *British Journal of Special Education*, 32(2): pp60–65.

Nind, M *et al.* (2003) *Inclusive education: diverse perspectives*. London: David Fulton.

Before you read the next extract prepare yourself by reading:

- Allan, J (2003) 'Productive pedagogies and the challenge of Inclusion'. *British Journal of Special Education*. 30(4): 175–9.
- Hanko, G (2003) 'Towards an inclusive school culture – but what happened to Elton's "affective curriculum"?' *British Journal of Special Education*, 30(3): 125–31.
- Lindsay, G (2003) 'Inclusive education: a critical perspective'. *British Journal of Special Education*, 30(1): 3–10.
- Tassoni, P (2003) *Supporting special needs: understanding inclusion in the early years*. Oxford: Heinemann.

Extract: Farrell, P (2001) 'Special education in the last twenty years: have things really got better?' *British Journal of Special Education*, 28(1): 7–8. Read 'Definitions of Inclusion'.

Definitions of inclusion

As most readers will know, up until the mid-1990s the term 'integration' rather than 'inclusion' was used. Integration typically referred solely to the type of setting into which a child might be placed, mainstream class, unit resource base, etc. One problem with defining integration in this way is that it tells us nothing about the quality of the education that is received in this provision. There have been examples where so-called 'integrated' placements have left the child being isolated and excluded from the many activities that take place in a school.

For this reason the term 'inclusion' has become a more accepted way of describing the extent to which a pupil with SEN is truly 'integrated'. Essentially the term refers to the extent to which a school or community welcomes all people as full members of the group and values them for the contribution which they make. For inclusion to be effective all pupils must actively belong to, be welcomed by and participate in a school and community – that is they should be fully *included*. Their diversity of interests, abilities and attainment should be welcomed and be seen to enrich the life of the school. See Booth and Ainscow (1998) and the Index for Inclusion (CSIE, 2000) for a more detailed elaboration of this view of inclusion.

Despite developments in thinking on inclusion that are reflected by these authors and several others, it is by no means clear that teachers, parents, LEA officers and DfEE officials think about inclusion in the same way. In the study carried out on behalf of the DfEE, referred to above, Ainscow *et al* (1999) found that LEA officers defined inclusion in a whole variety of ways, some of which appeared to be no different from earlier definitions of integration. I have also heard teachers proudly describe the fact that they now work in an 'inclusive school' purely because one or two pupils with physical difficulties have been placed there. More worryingly still, the new draft *Code Of Practice* seems to take a view of inclusion that is solely about placing pupils with SEN in mainstream schools and not about improving the practices that should take place within such schools to make them inclusive environments for all children. All of this suggests that there is much that needs to be done if we are to gain a consensus as to the definition of inclusion.

What are the arguments for inclusion?

As Mittler (2000) suggests, the main argument driving the inclusion movement has centred on the issue of human rights. It is argued that it is a basic right for all pupils to attend their mainstream school and be fully included in its academic and social processes. Any form of segregation is seen as a potential threat to the achievement of this basic right. The Centre for Studies in Inclusive Education (CSIE) has been energetically pursuing this line of argument for many years. It is also subsumed within the Salamanca Statement and, perhaps most importantly of all, the Government, through the Green Paper and the Programme of Action, also stresses the right of all children to attend a mainstream school if their parents wish it.

In my view arguments in favour of inclusion based solely on human rights, powerful though they may sound, are logically and conceptually naive (see Farrell, 1997, 2000). Surely, as Low (1997) argues, the basic right is for all pupils to receive a good education. Many parents might argue that this basic right can only be met if their child attends a special school, and that they should not be denied *their* right to choose such a school. There is also the question of whether respecting the rights of children with SEN by placing them in a mainstream school may pose a threat to the rights of their mainstream peers to receive a good education. These and other issues are discussed in more depth by Wilson (1999, 2000) who provides a detailed critique of the human rights perspective on inclusion.

There are, of course, a number of empirical arguments in favour of inclusion. For example, it is argued that pupils benefit socially and academically from being placed in a mainstream school and that their peer group develops a better understanding of disability. These and other arguments have the potential to inform developments in policy and practice although I would agree that the human rights perspective has probably been the most influential in moving things forward.

Are we all in favour of inclusion?

This question is complex and it is not easy to find an unequivocal answer. Clearly the numbers of pupils attending special schools has dropped over the last 20 years and now stands at around 1.3% (Howson, 2000). This seems to be explained by the rise in the numbers of pupils with physical and sensory difficulties attending mainstream provision, often in a resource base within the school. In addition, according to Cunningham, Glenn, Lorenz and Shepperdson (1998), between 70% and 80% of pupils with Down's syndrome now begin their education in a mainstream school. In order for these developments to have taken place it would appear that there has been a growth in the number of people who are now in favour of integration and possibly, therefore, inclusion. However, it is still the case that the vast majority of pupils with emotional and behavioural difficulties or severe and profound learning difficulties attend traditional special schools. There is also anecdotal evidence that some LEAs who attempt to reorganise their special provision find that they are faced with considerable opposition from parents, many of whom are concerned about the prospects for their children in a mainstream setting. In addition the teaching unions have expressed considerable disquiet at the prospect of the further inclusion of pupils with emotional and behavioural difficulties and some headteachers have expressed concern about the impact of inclusion on their school's position in national performance tables. Their concern is reinforced by the findings from a study by Norwich and Lunt (2000) who found a close association between schools with poor GCSE scores who also had high levels of Statementing and high percentages of pupils on stages 1 to 3 of the *Code of Practice*. All of this suggests that there are still powerful forces at work that are resisting further developments towards inclusion.

How?

How do you feel the inclusion agenda, with particular reference to SEN, has evolved since 2001?

In the earlier sections of this chapter, legislation and guidance implemented post 2001 have been discussed in detail with regard to SEN. You have been in the fortunate position to be or have recently been, a trainee teacher visiting schools where there is evidence of good practice and experienced teachers to observe and learn from. This chapter has given you the theoretical underpinnings to be able to evaluate your experiences to date and to utilise all this information and experience to enable you to develop skills and ways of thinking about special educational needs and inclusive practice that will influence your developing professional career. Have you experienced changes in special educational needs practices and are these supporting the needs of the individual children as well as/or in spite of/instead of the inclusion policy framework? How has the role of the SENCO changed within the last few years?

Why?

Why is the definition of inclusion so vital to the development of practice within schools and to SEN?

Many definitions of inclusion can be found in journals and books and it depends on when it was written, the background and experiences of the author and the professional role they fulfil. I suggest, however, that if equality of services is going to be achieved nationally, an acceptable definition of inclusive practice needs to be acknowledged by government as the baseline from which school communities can gauge their progress. In this way schools can evaluate their own progress and ensure that all their pupils, including those with special educational needs are having their learning and social needs met. Without clear direction, to be evaluated at times of inspection, pupils, especially those with special educational needs will 'slip through the net' while change is occurring, especially if their traditional 'champion', the SENCO, is no longer involved in ensuring the SEN Code of Practice is being implemented at the practice level.

What?

What impact has inclusion had on the class teacher? Which area of need has required the greatest amount of support to enable teachers to develop appropriate skills and working practices?

Teachers have proved to be very amenable and capable of managing change and methods of practice since the introduction of the National Curriculum. However, there have been great concerns raised about the feasibility of managing and educating certain pupils with particular needs within an inclusive classroom. Additional training and active support is being carried out to try to raise the confidence levels of teachers with regards to these areas of need. It is not surprising that inclusion has had a huge impact on the practitioners; not only do they have to learn to adapt their curriculum, their methods of teaching and planning, but they also have to undergo additional training to be able to engage with pupils with many SEN needs they know little about. Are the government and academics listening to the needs of the teachers, particularly SEN concerns, as well as the pupils?

Personal response

Read the following quotation, keeping the role of the SENCO as described by the *National Standards for Special Educational Needs Co-ordinators* (TTA, 1998) and of special educational needs legislation, *SEN Code of Practice* (2001) clearly in mind. Remember schools still need to pay regard to these and execute the legal duties described for those children with the greatest level of special educational needs:

More inclusive schools will have more inclusive management arrangements with greater sharing of the (SENCO) role. Indeed, the most inclusive schools may have moved away from SEN provision altogether and be fostering more reflective mechanisms which support the development of pedagogy at the classroom/department level.

(Moore, 1999, p177)

Critically examine how this has/can be achieved in practice, remembering the developments that have occurred at the local level during the past two or three years. Argue for or against the dismantling of SEN provision and the effect it has had on teachers.

Practical implications and activities

1. With a colleague formulate a simple table to illustrate the possible changes in primary schools with regard to SEN and inclusion for the last six years, utilising legislation, guidance and literature to identify key words and phrases. Evaluate your findings to demonstrate whether greater changes have occurred:
   • affecting the educational aspects of a child's experience of school;
   OR
   • the social/community aspects of a child's experience of school.

2. Critically examine your findings from the activity above, focusing on what aspect of a school community has had to alter/change its practice to enable the inclusive practice to be successfully implemented. Has this change involved parents, the LEA, support staff, teachers, or other adults and pupils? Why do you suspect this aspect of a school's ethos and practice has adapted to change more easily than others?

   Having gathered all your findings together draw up a list of ten hypothetical questions you would like to ask a school about why it made certain changes and not others. Ask your colleague to construct possible answers, again using documentary and theoretical evidence, as well as experience to inform the responses made. Debate with a number of colleagues about the conclusions reached.

3. What have you learnt about teaching in a school adapting to the current inclusive framework from these activities?

   How will this help you to be an active team member of the school community?

Further reading

Blandford, S (2005a) *Sonia Blandford's Masterclass*. London: Sage.

Corbett, J (1999) 'Inclusive education and school culture'. *International Journal of Inclusive Education*, 3(1): 53–61.

Croll, P and Moses, D (2000) 'Ideologies and utopias: education professionals' views of inclusion'. *European Journal of Special Needs Education*, 15(1): 1–12.

Moore, J (1999) 'Developing a local authority response to inclusion'. *Support for Learning*, 14(4): 174–178.

Wedell, K (2000) 'Putting "inclusion" into practice'. Points from the SENCO-Forum. *British Journal of Special Education*, 27(2): 100.

Section 2
Working with Others

5 Working in partnership with parents and carers

By the end of this chapter you should have considered, analysed and reflected upon:

- **why** it is necessary for you to explore and examine your views and attitudes about working in *partnership* with parents and carers;
- **what** legislation, research and underpinning theory can help you engage with this issue in a positive manner, to support learning, behaviour and pastoral development in your classroom;
- **how** your understanding and ability to really engage with partnerships with parents and carers can have a significant effect upon the learning and expectations of the pupils you teach.

Linking your learning
Achieving QTS: Professional studies primary phase, second edition, Jacques, K and Hyland, R (2003) Chapter 12.

Professional Standards for QTS
1.4, 1.5, 2.4, 3.2.7

Introduction

Working in partnership with parents and carers is an important area of current interest and development within the government's agenda for inclusion for all pupils; and it is one that is of particular significance for pupils who have special educational needs. The *Special Educational Needs Code of Practice* (DfES, 2001b, 2:2, p16) states clearly:

> The work of professionals can be more effective when parents are involved and account is taken of their wishes, feelings and perspectives on their children's development . . . All parents of children with special educational needs should be treated as partners.

It also states that a great deal of support and positive attitudes by the professionals may be required as these relationships can be challenging. Indeed it may be because of such difficulties that many parent partnerships remain very superficial and are not always considered by teachers as a necessary part of developing good practice, let alone essential practice in schools. Professionals' personal family experiences, social skills required to relate with adults, lack of confidence and time are also undoubtedly factors that determine teachers' views and willingness to engage with developing effective parent partnerships.

Prior to the Plowden Report (CACE, 1967), and I would argue even up until more recently in many cases, parents were generally not welcome visitors in school, with the school gates designating the separation of school and the outside world. With changing social structures and the need for transparency in all work practices 'allowing' and 'asking for information' from parents and carers has gradually been identified as useful for schools and teachers in meeting the needs of pupils, especially those with very individual and different needs. With the publication of *Every child matters* (HMSO, 2003) and the Children Act (HMSO, 2004) the government has signalled its determination to take partnership working much further than ever before, believing that within this new framework it will be possible to achieve the aim *to transform outcomes for children* (*TES*, May 20, 2005, p24). The government has also promised to take action to *spread best practice in improving accountability to parents for SEN and in providing advice and support to parents locally* (DfES, 2004, p73).

Many very bold statements are being presented to teachers in recent documentation and literature. For example, Human Scale Education says: *there is much evidence to suggest that schools which have a high level of parental involvement are more successful* (HSE, 2005) and the SEN Code of Practice (DfES, 2001b in OFSTED, 2004, p3) includes as one of its five principles *that parents have a vital role to play in supporting their children's education*. It is therefore vital that you, as a trainee teacher really considers seriously what this means for you both as an individual and as a new professional. We all have our own 'history' and it is important that this is recognised, reflected upon and issues arising resolved so that when you find yourself, as a new professional, in a situation that involves complicated partnership working you can recognise and effectively deal with possible prejudices and personally held beliefs. Without this insight your expectations and willingness to 'go that extra mile' for individual pupils may be coloured by your own experiences and what your relationship with their parents/carers are like. How many times have you heard already 'Well what do you expect when they live in that environment?' Nobody is denying, that there appears to be unified thinking that, *parenting has a strong impact on a child's educational development, behaviour and mental health* (HMSO, 2003, p39). Clearly leaving it at this point is no longer acceptable practice. Schools are now being asked to keep working with parents in as many ways as possible to enable the development of meaningful, real partnerships within the educational environment. You therefore need to examine truthfully what you think about working with parents in schools. Additionally do you feel you have the skills and confidence to collaborate and build working relationships with the parents and carers? Don't forget it is very different working with children to working with adults and many teachers, in my own personal experience, will 'go to jelly' if they have to talk to/work with other adults. Further reading and discussion with colleagues and peers will help you build a firm foundation for answering the questions: 'Why is parental partnership so important for pupil learning?' and, 'What do you need to do if issues are preventing your ability to become willing to develop your professional skills in this area'?

Before you read the following extract, prepare yourself by reading:

- Carnie, F (2005) *Pathways to child friendly schools: a guide for parents.* HSE.
- DfES, (2001b) *Special Educational Needs Code of Practice*, Chapter 2, pp16–26. Annesley: DfES.
- Gibson, S and Blandford, S (2005) *Managing special educational needs.* London: Paul Chapman Publishing.

Extract: Thacker, J Stradwick, D and Babbedge, E (2002) *Educating children with emotional and behavioural difficulties – inclusive practice in mainstream schools*, pp107, 111–113, 115. London: Routledge Falmer.

Expectations
As mentioned in the previous chapter school systems may carry their own expectations of groups that are perceived as problematic.

Sometimes teachers may stop making an effort or just expect, because they work within a difficult catchment area, that you can't do or achieve some things with 'our children'. Demographic features do have an effect but these should not be used as an excuse for not exploring other courses of action. Similarly, in apparently well-functioning groups personal and social education is equally relevant.

In a culture that often blames teachers or parents for the short-comings of the society, it is important that schools don't pass on such blaming tactics themselves – *or* fall into the trap of labelling groups of parents or particular parents.

Is a change of school indicated?
School and home can get to the point where they are not communicating and everything seems to be going wrong for all concerned. For some parents in this situation, a change of school may seem the only option. Frightened parents can do the proverbial 'moonlight flit' and disappear without warning, hoping to give their child and themselves a fresh start with no historical baggage. Others can arrive at the new school and heap mountains of blame on the place they have just left. Thus the parents of some challenging children can move from school to school, never allowing difficulties to be faced and worked through. How much better for the child, parents and school if all can gain confidence and effect changes for the child in partnership together.

However, in some cases, a change of school can be beneficial. The child and his/her parents may feel that the new school will be more understanding. We have already quoted the example (see p20) of the headteacher who surprised and delighted the parents of a boy with EBD by saying that the child would be 'a gift to the school'. This set a positive tone for the placement, and the child, as we reported, made great strides in learning and behaviour in that school.

Coping with difficult situations
It is extremely hard to stay focused and calm when an irate or threatening parent is facing you at the classroom door because they have a concern about their child or the school. It goes against our instincts of 'fight or flight' which make us want to turn our

backs on the problem or put up our fists, actually or metaphorically, to defend ourselves and maybe return a blow or two in the process. As teachers we may quite often be in the firing line and we need to learn how to handle ourselves professionally. When parents come into school ready to fight their corner for their child they may have insufficient information or even the wrong information. Parents, for a range of reasons, may feel extremely threatened and vulnerable about having to come into the school at difficult times. Which of us, when feeling like that, can put forward our best side and be rational and reasonable? In such circumstances, it is helpful if one of the parties knows something about resolving problems productively and peacefully, and this should be a part of the professional teacher's repertoire.

Why?

Why is it so important to foster effective partnerships with parents/carers of pupils with special educational needs?

Many parents/carers of pupils with special educational needs still, in a great number of cases, have to be very proactive and 'fight' for what type of education and support they feel their child requires. They may also feel threatened or are indeed very vulnerable and might have their own challenges that mean they need even more support to help their children. Therefore it is important for pupils' confidence and for learning potential that parents also gain confidence and belief in the teachers and school. Your initial contact and manner in which you introduce yourself, listen to and answer their questions and welcome their child is therefore vital as a trainee/class teacher. Don't forget that the parents/carers are the ones that see their role as 'fighting their child's corner'. However if good partnerships are formed the outcomes can be beneficial for the pupil, parents/carers and teachers and everyone will work towards a joint goal.

Parents/carers know their child better than anyone else in the majority of cases. If systems/support structures are well considered you as a teacher can be given vital information and understanding of pupils' strengths, needs and also strategies to overcome various problems involving perhaps communication and behaviour issues. This is unquestionably a more significant factor for pupils with special educational needs than for others. The way in which schools and individual teachers approach this is very important and can obviously develop or hamper successful partnerships. Many schools, for example, will say they keep in daily contact with parents of pupils with SEN through diaries, and hold this up as good parental partnership (and in many cases it is a very positive manner in which to communicate, especially for more severely disabled pupils), but who writes in them and what is included in them is a vital factor determining whether this is true or not. Consider who you have seen completing such a book and what is actually told to the parent/carer. You may think this has little to do with developing a good working partnership, but if a parent regularly receives a book that is filled out by a support member of staff and with misbehaviours, problems and little regard for what they had written in it, perhaps identifying reasons for lack of homework, it will form a barrier to real cooperation. This book communicates to the parent/carer that:

- their child has been a behaviour problem in the class (yet again);
- their child does not work hard, cannot do the work;
- their comments are not listened to or appropriately responded to;
- their child is not very well liked by the teacher (and/or peers);
- they and their child are not valued members of the school community.

An immediate effect of this may be the parent/carer stops communicating with the teacher and also feels there needs to be a 'them and us' approach when they are invited for meetings. The teacher is also putting the blame for the pupils difficulties squarely on the shoulders of the parent/carer and not accepting some of the load him/herself. You can see the harm this does for pupils learning, self-esteem and respect for the teachers and school.

This clearly demonstrates the importance of every teacher within a school community engaging with systems that are put in place to enable effective partnership. If you, even as a trainee teacher, do not learn to really listen to and value parent input and how to best communicate the difficulties a pupil may be experiencing and the strengths of course, it can cause a great loss of trust and cooperation that could well make your work more difficult and will almost certainly affect the way in which a pupil values his/her school work and therefore learning. For pupils with special educational needs this may impact on regular government requirements such as collaborative working with IEPs and Annual Reviews and could really make important decision-making about transitions and different provision into confrontational events between parents and teachers. This consequently could have a long-term effect on a pupil's educational and social success. Trust and working practices, just like any other partnership, take a long time to establish, but only one thoughtless word or action to ruin.

How?

How can you develop the systems and skills to establish real parent partnerships?

The whole school ethos regarding parent partnership is vital to help you build and establish the skills you will require so that you will be able to *resolve problems productively and peacefully* (Thacker et al, 2002, p115), *but* you also need to understand why and how this can be achieved. The Parent's Charter (DfEE, 1991; updated 1994) and new forms of parental involvement, such as the home-school 'contracts of partnership' (agreements) written in the government White Paper, *Excellence in cities* (DfEE, 1998) in which schools are obliged to listen and respond to parental opinion (Crozier and Reay, 2005). Schools and parents are now jointly responsible for helping pupils learning, but have they really altered the power imbalance between schools and homes about educational decision making?

Again this is particularly significant for pupils with special educational needs who are perhaps attending a mainstream provision where knowledge of a specific need is limited. Would you feel comfortable and confident enough to frequently ask a parent for information and assistance with one of your pupils? If not, why not? Have your feelings any real supporting reasons? Perhaps you feel the pupil shouldn't even be attending a mainstream provision, but the parent/carer has exercised his/her right to choose a school. What problems need to be overcome in this type of situation? The important factor here is to hold the needs of the pupil central to any discussions. It is not helpful to hold an 'I know best' stance, without really engaging in discussions about the pupil's educational needs.

With the support of the school and of the special educational needs co-ordinator (SENCO) particularly, additional training, ways of working and support structures in the classroom will need to be considered in close liaison with other agencies and the parents. If the parents can see that the school, and the class teacher specifically, are willing to adapt their practice to meet the needs of their child, without negative educational effects on others in the classroom, the decision-making for the provision of the educational needs of this pupil is not being taken away from the school, but rather being enhanced by the parents and other agencies. Hence a trusting, effective way of working is established and in such an environment if there are times when a school is experiencing tremendous problems it is far more likely that the parents will support the school as an informed and equal partner. In this way an aim of *Every child matters* (HMSO, 2003, 2.17, 28) *to ensure that parents have the confidence that their children's needs will be met quickly and effectively throughout their education* can be achieved in a positive way for all.

If a teacher just expects a pupil to work alongside others and is unwilling, because of personally held beliefs and feelings, to consider individual needs then when problems arise the parents may question the amount of investment really given to their child and thus work against the school.

What?

What you implement will therefore be very dependent on the school ethos, the needs of the parents, but most importantly they will have to meet the needs of the pupils so that they can learn in a positive environment with high expectations of their learning. As a trainee teacher it is vital that you begin to develop skills that will enable you to work effectively with parents, as the professional in an equal partnership holding the pupils needs as the main criteria for any action.

Personal response

Explore and analyse your real feelings about working with parents/carers as equal partners. Discuss with a colleague any concerns/worries about working in this way and debate whether the issues raised have genuine, well evidenced reasons, or whether they are a response to:

- your own experience as a pupil;
- your experience as a parent;
- your professional experience or as a result of listening to other colleagues;
- insecurities about your own knowledge or experience?

Practical implications and activities

- Parent/carer partnership is unquestionably an important part of the government's education agenda. Read the legislation and guidance listed below and then critically evaluate how the government's intentions to support mainstream class teachers in mastering additional knowledge and skills, will impact on the quality of parent/carer partnerships for you as a new member of the teaching profession.

1. DfES, (2004) *Removing barriers to achievement – the government's strategy for SEN*. Annesley: DfES.
2. DfES, (2001b) *Special Educational Needs Code of Practice*, Chapter 2, 2:1–2:31, pp16–25. Annesley: DfES.
3. DfES (2001a) *Inclusive schooling*. Annesley: DfES.
4. OFSTED (2004) *Special Educational Needs and Disability*. London: OFSTED.
5. HMSO, (2003) *Every child matters*. Norwich: HMSO.

- Which member of staff within a school will you particularly need to work closely with when meeting with parents/carers of pupils with special educational needs? How can this member of staff assist you especially when you are a trainee or newly qualified teacher?
- Discuss and examine, with a colleague or team, how good practice in working with parents/carers whose children have special educational needs can inform and enhance practice throughout the school.

Further reading

Blandford, S (2005a) *Sonia Blandford's Masterclass*. London: Sage.

Blandford, S (2005b) *Remodelling in schools: workforce reform*. London: Pearson.

Crozier, G and Reay, D (2005) *Activating participation*. Stoke on Trent: Trentham Books Ltd.

Constable, D (2002) *Planning and organising the SENCO year*. London: David Fulton.

Beveridge, S (2005) *Children, families and schools: developing partnerships for inclusive education*. London: RoutledgeFalmer.

Look at:

www.teachernet.gov.uk/sen

www.hse.org.uk/pwp/partnership.html

Before you read the next extract, prepare yourself by reading:

- Farrell, P (2001) 'Special education in the last twenty years: have things really got better? *British Journal of Special Education*, 28, (1): 3–9.
- Rix, J (2003) A parent's wish-list, in Nind, M, Rix, J, Sheehy, K and Simmons, K (2003) *Inclusive education: diverse perspectives*. London: David Fulton in association with The Open University.

Extract: Riddell, S (2000) 'Inclusion and choice: mutually exclusive principles in special educational needs', in Armstrong, F, Armstrong, D and Barton, L (eds) *Inclusive education – policy, contexts and comparative perspectives*. London: David Fulton.

Tensions between choice and integration/inclusion: how parents negotiate the system

There appeared to be marked variation among parents between those who were able to articulate their choice of school with professionals and those who were not able to do this. Generally, parents who were able to persuade professionals of the validity of their claims were middle class. The salience of social class was illustrated in relation to two children with Down's syndrome, Brian who was placed in mainstream for his primary education, and Tony who was placed in special. Even though Brian's pre-school psychological assessment was rather negative, his professional mother and father argued strongly that their son should spend the early years of his education in the local village primary. His mother explained:

> 'Middleton is a relatively small place and my husband and I didn't see why Brian should be bussed out of the area until he's about 16 and then arrive back here and nobody knows him. Whereas now we go down to the town and it's 'Hi Brian, hi Brian'. He goes to Sunday school and boys' brigade.'

The Record of Needs provided testimony of professional approval of the parents, who were described as 'intelligent caring people who have provided a richly stimulating home environment for him. They are anxious to pursue a positive approach which has obviously contributed greatly to Brian's development.' The head teacher was in no doubt as to why Brian's parents had been successful in countering the psychologist's argument that the boy would be better off in special:

> 'I think really it is only because they are very well educated, articulate people that they are able to fight their case. I'm sure had they been people who had easily been put down or pushed aside things would have gone in the other direction. I would say they knew their rights and fought their case and that is why Brian is still here.'

Both the headteacher and the class teacher were still doubtful about the success of the placement, feeling that Brian would have got 'something special' (although they were not sure what that might have been) in a special school. Although Brian's parents had won the fight for an integrated placement in primary school, they had, somewhat reluctantly, agreed to a placement in a special unit attached to a mainstream secondary for Brian's secondary education:

> 'It would be great if there was a unit in Middleton Academy, then he could go on with the children he knows, but unfortunately not, so it's out of the question. I feel a bit concerned that he'll see a lot of handicapped children … Johnson is really the best of a bad bunch.'

By way of contrast, Tony, from a working class background, started his educational career in a school for children with moderate learning difficulties and was subsequently transferred to a school for pupils with severe learning difficulties. At the time of the interview, Tony was 15, and, looking back, his mother wished that she had insisted on an integrated placement:

'I never ever tried to get Tony into a normal school. Sometimes I wish I had but then I felt that kids were cruel and I was frightened. I didn't know how Tony was going to turn out. Looking at him now, I wish I had tried to get him into a normal school.'

Having three sons close together, she had always treated Tony the same as her other boys. In the eyes of the psychologist, this represented both a potential problem because it indicated a failure to recognise Tony's problems. The psychologist's assessment in the Record of Needs recognised the affectionate and caring nature of Tony's home, but continued:

Difficulties have arisen because of Tony's lack of progress in formal schoolwork. Mrs M has been very frustrated by this and is struggling to come to terms with the cognitive limitations of Tony's handicap and her need to change her approach to him ... Until Mrs M adjusts to the limitations of Tony's cognitive ability she may well be disappointed with his progress at Budmouth [school for children with severe learning difficulties].

Mrs M was still indignant that her refusal to treat Tony as 'an ill person' had been seen as abnormal by the psychologist, but despite her indignation she had seen no alternative but to acquiesce with professional judgements.

Among our case studies it was evident that choice represented a strategy strongly dependent on social class. However, middle class parents did not always wish for their child to be educated in mainstream. In Authority E, another of our case studies was of Catherine, a girl with Down's Syndrome about to enter secondary. Her mother was adamant that she did not wish a placement in a special base because her daughter might be in danger from the other children and would not get enough specialist input. Although the authority was trying to close the special school which Catherine's mother wished her to attend, the placing request was acceded to.

Geography and the established pattern of local authority provision were also factors influencing Tony and Brian's placements. Living in an urban area with many special schools, a mainstream placement for Tony might have been seen as distorting the authority's budget because of the need to resource two distinctive types of provision. For Brian, living in a rural area, placement in a mainstream primary with additional support might have been seen as a cheaper option than a special school placement which would have involved the cost of transport. Furthermore, although children with certain 'types' of SEN were liable to be placed in either mainstream or special settings, those with profound or multiple difficulties were almost invariably placed in special settings irrespective of the parents' social class, the authority's geography, policy and established pattern of provision.

Conclusion

Tensions between the principles of integration/inclusion and choice have characterised special educational needs policy in the UK for two decades. Comparing special educational needs policy documents of the 1970s and early 1990s, we find a shift away from the idea of partnership with parents towards the notion of parents as consumers, albeit less powerful than parents of non-disabled children. Integration, identified by Warnock as the favoured option, occupies a less prominent position in Conservative special educational needs policy, despite strong lobbying by the disability movement. New Labour policy documents in England herald a decisive shift towards integration/inclusion.

Case study data provide insight into how parents of children with special educational needs experienced the twin principles of integration and choice. It was evident that a pure market did not exist within which parents were free to choose between integrated and segregated options. Rather, choice was structured by regional policy, geography, social class and nature of the child's impairment. Ball (1993) maintained that the implementation of market reforms in education is essentially 'a class strategy which has as one of its major effects the reproduction of relative social class (and ethnic) advantages and disadvantages' (p4). In the sphere of special educational needs, it is evident that opportunities are structured not only by social class but by a much wider range of factors including the nature of the child's impairment.

Tensions between integration and choice within special educational needs policy 'reveal an underlying tension between individualism and collectivism. The previous Conservative government almost always came down on the side of individualism, although, as Jonathan (1993) noted:

> A market in education creates a competitive framework in which parents as consumers can seek relative advantage for their children. But it also creates a situation in which each child becomes vulnerable to the unspecifiable effects of the aggregate choices of other children's proxies. (p21)

In special educational needs, this is particularly apparent. If parents reject special schools, these swiftly become too expensive to run. By the same token, investment in the infrastructure of mainstream depends on enough parents choosing this option.

Why?

Why do parent partnerships have such an important role to play in raising achievement and enhancing learning for pupils with special educational needs?

Parents have that one important element that is so valuable for a pupil with special educational needs – a love and a belief in them and a 'need' to 'get them the best education they can'. As a trainee teacher it is helpful to remember this when meeting with parents and wise to acknowledge the parents' knowledge and experience of the pupil. This powerful force can be channelled by you as the teacher in a way that encourages learning and supports your teaching if collaboration is sought or if rejected it can disempower the pupil as a learner and thus you as a teacher. As Rix (2003, p82–3) says:

> The teacher inside me sees the parent wanting to have his cake and eat it. But as a parent that is exactly what I do want . . . The Special Educational Needs Co-ordinator and outside bodies will hopefully step in to help supply the appropriate information that can be passed on in the classroom. As a parent I believe I should also take some responsibility for this and should pass on to the school my understanding of Robbie . . . I hope to work with the school in partnership. It must not be about confrontation or dogma, but should be a flexible and open relationship, with Robbie as the focus.

Parents/carers can assist a school when dealing with behaviour, communication, dietary issues and even curriculum matters and in this way the triangle of influence on pupils is complete. There is no splitting between parent, pupil and teacher and successful learning remains everyone's main focus point.

The government states that research has informed them that *parental involvement in education seems to be a more important influence than poverty, school environment and the influence of peers* (HMSO, 2003, p18).

How?

Do you think there is still an inequality of service for parents of children with special educational needs and if so, *how* can you ensure your practice does not support such actions?

The extract above clearly identifies an inequality of decision-making and opportunity for two pupils, due mostly to the parents' level of knowledge of the education system and their confidence in voicing their opinion against this system. Indeed the decisions taken may well have affected the learning and therefore life chances of Tony.

As a trainee teacher you need to examine and explore ways in which your practice can ensure all the pupils within your care can receive the same chances to achieve. This does not mean all pupils need exactly the same experiences or methods of schooling or interventions, but it does mean the opportunity to receive a 'different' more appropriate education should be the same for all those requiring it. For those parents without the means or knowledge to access information or to 'work the system' a true partnership would ensure all the facts were fairly and professionally discussed. By providing information, support and direction to parents/carers and by actively valuing their opinions and concerns, all the parties involved in a child's educational welfare can determine within a professional and proactive atmosphere what the best course of action is for the pupil at that particular stage of his/her educational experience.

What?

What can schools do to foster such partnerships for the benefit of the pupil, parents/carers and the school itself?

First it is important to understand that like any other partnership there must be a willingness from all parties to compromise, listen and respect others' points of view. With this in mind it is imperative that teachers and schools have the commitment to this way of working. As Mittler (2000, p153) says: *Every school needs its own home – school policy to go beyond fine words and include concrete proposals for achieving better working relationships with its parents and the local community.*

A number of new initiatives the government are introducing can be seen as attempts to ensure that every pupil receives equality of opportunity and that schools are to be seen as a focal point for all the community and not just pupils and teachers. The *extended schools agenda* (DfES, 2005) and funded projects such as the 'Working for Change in your Child's School' (HSE, **www.hse.org.uk/pwp/partnership.html**, downloaded 25.05.2005) have been supported to encourage real collaborative working. A willingness to see pupils' teaching and learning as of concern to all involved in their welfare will enable teachers and schools to creatively develop ways of working that supports everyone and also improves academic performance (Beveridge, 2005).

Personal response

1. Reflect on your own personal or professional experiences of home – school working for a pupil with special educational needs. Do you feel that collaborative working helped or would have supported the pupil in question achieve a greater level of academic success? Examine your responses and using recent legislation, guidance and literature critically evaluate the role the school, the class teacher and the parent /carer played in the decision-making process.
2. Why do you, as a trainee teacher, believe the government is emphasising the need for the development of parent partnerships? Discuss with a colleague positive reasons for close collaboration with parents/carers for:
   * pupils;
   * schools;
   * and for the whole community and thus society.

   Map your results on a table. Do you notice any factors that reoccur across all the sectors? Do you think that this reason may have influenced the government's decision in determining policy and practice?

Practical implications and activities

Examine in detail the policies and practices with regard to parent partnership of one school you have worked in as a trainee teacher for the pupils with special educational needs. Comment and reflect on your answers to the questions below asking yourself 'How do I know?' and 'What did I see that confirmed this?':

1. Was there a real 'open door' policy for parents of children with special educational needs?
2. Were the parents just invited to meetings about their child's special educational needs, or was real collaborative practice in place?
3. Who were the real decision makers?
4. Were parents always fully informed of all the options for their child even if it might mean extra financial commitment from either themselves, the school or the Local Education Authority?
5. Were the parents/carers kept regularly informed of all the strategies/interventions the class teacher, perhaps yourself, tried to improve the pupil's access and engagement in the curriculum?
6. Was the parent/carer voice really listened to, respected and acted upon?

Further reading

Beveridge, S (2005) *Children, families and schools: developing partnerships for inclusive education*. London: RoutledgeFalmer.

Blamires, M and Moore, J (2003) *Support services and mainstream schools: a guide for working together*. London: David Fulton.

Gibson, S and Blandford, S (2005) *Managing special educational needs*. London: Paul Chapman.

Greenwood, C (2002) *Understanding the needs of parents: guidelines for effective collaboration with parents of children with special educational needs*. London: David Fulton.

Mittler, P (2000) *Working towards inclusive education: social contexts*. London: David Fulton.

South East Region SEN Partnership (undated) *Working positively with parents*. Filsham Valley School: Michael Phillips.

Vincent, C (2004) *Including parents*. Berkshire: Open University.

6 Working in partnership with other agencies

By the end of this chapter you should have considered and reflected upon:

- **why** you need to understand the roles and responsibilities of professionals from other agencies, the background to joint agency working and the positive impact collaborative working can have for pupils;
- **what** transferable skills and working methods you will require to be able to work effectively with other professionals in order to support your pupils learning and social needs;
- **how** working with professionals from other agencies can enhance and broaden your skills as a teacher and also enable you to share your skills with others.

Linking your learning
Achieving QTS: Professional studies primary phase, second edition, Jacques, K and Hyland, R (2003) Chapter 12.

Professional Standards for QTS
1.6, 3.2.7

Introduction

It is first necessary to ensure you are aware of the background to the development of joint agency working. It is one area that, for many reasons, has required government pressure to be considered seriously as a vital part of daily working practice for the teaching profession. This development is also of particular intrinsic interest to all those working with pupils with special educational needs.

Thirty-five years ago Bronfenbrenner (1970) highlighted the need for legislation to facilitate effective inter-agency working for the benefit of children. Despite many changes during the past three decades, the construct of the medical model used for implementing special educational needs policy and practice has meant that the professional roles of the various statutory agencies have remained isolated. Consequently the services provided for pupils with special educational needs have frequently been fragmented, causing waste of resources, repetition of services and unco-ordinated provision to support learning. Hence when the inclusion agenda began to gain momentum in schools, the possibilities for real collaborative working had to be taken forward initially by individual schools, health workers and social workers.

The Children Act (1989) and the Education Act (1996) placed on schools, health, social services and LEAs the requirement to help each other if requested. Then in 2001 the *Special Educational Needs Code of Practice* (DfES, 2001b) and the *SEN Toolkit, Sections 11 and 12* (DfES, 2001c:4) emphasised the roles of the statutory agencies to work together and began to include language such as *close collaboration* (DfES, 2001c: 12, 4) and *flexible working* (DfES, 2001c:135, 10.1). However, it was through the Green Paper *Every child matters* (HMSO, 2003) that the government demonstrated in a radical manner their commitment to inclusion by stating that they were going to legislate to achieve their aim of integrating services to enable a child focused approach to education and care. Indeed *Removing barriers to achievement – the government's strategy for SEN* (2004) clearly identifies these aims and illustrates how they are going to be achieved. Children with special educational needs are an important factor in the government's eagerness to encourage joint agency working to aid improvements in the provision of education and social care.

Before you read the following extract, prepare yourself by reading:

- Bronfenbrenner, U (1970) *Two worlds of childhood: US and USSR*. New York: Sage.
- Lacey, P (2001) *Support partnerships: collaboration in action*. London: David Fulton.

Extract: Soan, S (2004) 'Inter-agency collaboration and partnership with parents: roles and responsibilities', pp13–14, in Soan, S *Additional educational needs – inclusive approaches to teaching*. London: David Fulton.

Introduction

With the inclusion agenda gaining momentum, it seems the most logical action for practitioners in schools is to work closely with colleagues from other agencies, support services, voluntary services and charities. The National Curriculum Inclusion Statement (DfEE, 1999) and the SEN Code of Practice (DfES, 2001) reinforce this statement. The latter of these documents dedicates whole chapters to 'Working in partnership with parents', 'Pupil participation' and 'Working in partnership with other agencies', emphasising the importance now placed on joined-up thinking. In the first section of the 'Working in partnership with other agencies' chapter it states: 'Meeting the special educational needs of individual children requires flexible working on the part of the statutory agencies. They need to communicate and agree policies and protocols that ensure there is a 'seamless' service' (DfES, 2001: 135, 10.1). This, to the majority of people, is a reasonable and obvious avenue of development to pursue, to further enhance a holistic support system for children and young people. However, to enable this development to reach fruition it is considered necessary for the government to pass legislation to facilitate such action. Indeed, Bronfenbrenner stated such a necessity in 1970:

> It is a sobering fact that, neither in our communities nor in the nation as a whole, is there a single agency that is charged with the responsibility of assessing or improving the situation of the child in his total environment. As it stands, the needs of children are parcelled out among a hopeless confusion of agencies ... no one ... is concerned with the total pattern of life in the community.
>
> (1970:163)

Roaf (2002) also supports this point of view and suggests that legislation, organisation, professional practice and resources are the four main factors that contribute to the success of inter-agency work. She writes: 'legislation should also devise effective government structures which do not compartmentalise children and ensure that preventative and proactive work is fully integrated' (ibid.: 146).

However, it was not until the Green Paper, *Every Child Matters* that the government's intention to integrate the key services within a single organisational focus at both local and national levels in England and Wales was demonstrated. At the national level, the government aims to do this through a number of initiatives, such as a new Children's Commissioner who will act as an independent champion, and 'in the long term, integrate key services for children and young people under the Director of Children's Services as part of Children's Trusts' (HMSO, 2003). At the local level the government will *encourage* this joint working by setting out practice standards expected of each agency, ensuring children are a priority across services and involving and listening to children's and young people's views. Three other factors clearly identify the government's determination to ensure that joint working is developed further. They are:

- rationalising performance targets, plans, funding streams, financial accountability and indicators;
- creating an integrated inspection framework for children's services. OFSTED will take the lead in bringing together joint inspection teams. This will ensure services are judged on how they work together.
- creating an improvement and intervention function to improve performance by sharing effective practice, and intervening where services are failing. (HMSO, 2003)

The practice nevertheless can be very different from the theory, as Lacey's (2001) research on inter-professional work within a special school found. In this situation Lacey concluded that the attempt to collaborate with other agencies caused anxiety and even hostility. Referring to the definitions of 'anxiety' and 'hostility' within the psychology of personal constructs (Kelly, 1955), Blamires and Moore write:

Anxiety is defined as the awareness of an individual that she may not have the skills, knowledge or understanding required to deal with a forthcoming event or challenge, whilst hostility is the active refusal to adapt to the implications of forthcoming events or challenges.

(2003:7)

Why?

Why has it taken this level of government intervention to enable what seems a sensible and logical move to really be initiated?

As suggested in the article there are a number of reasons why collaborative working has not succeeded in practice, except in a few cases, until quite recently. The ability to

pool financial resources has been a great difficulty with agencies refusing to contribute towards a child's needs due to the fact that, looked at in isolation, 'A' has
'nothing to do with the health of the child' for example. Time, training and an understanding of the roles and responsibilities of the various statutory authorities have also
been limited and in many ways still restrict some effective collaboration working. With
recent initiatives, guidance and legislation the physical and financial barriers to these
issues are being removed and a monitoring and inspection system is to be introduced
to 'encourage' the changes and developments (HMSO, 2003, 5.36, 5.38:76).

> The government is committed to ensuring inspection captures how well services
> work together to improve children's lives within a framework that is consistent with
> the recommendations of the recent Office for Public Services Reform review. To do
> this, we intend to create an integrated inspection framework across children's ser-
> vices. Ofsted will take the lead…
>
> Inspections would lead to a published report which would assess and give a rating
> for the quality of provision overall, as well as service by service and also the quality
> of joint working such as information sharing and multi-disciplinary teams.
>
> (HMSO, 2003, 5.36, 5.38: 76)

For children with special educational needs *Removing barriers to achievement* (DfES,
2004) also emphasises this determination to interlock resources, professional expertise
and training: *We want to see: greater integration of education, health and social care
to meet the needs of children and families in line with the proposals set out in Every
child matters'* (DfES, 2004:72)

How?

How will such radical ways of working succeed?

There are very few people who would dispute that a policy that puts the needs of children at the heart of all the services is to be praised and supported. However, when
individual and professional identity appear to be threatened by developments in policy
there needs to be considerable support and training provided if effective moves forward
are to be achieved. Quite correctly I believe, you would most probably say that professional identity and the fear of losing job security are two major reasons why true
inter-agency working has taken so long to develop. The fear of not being able to cope
with the changes and new skills required, as research carried out by Lacey (2001)
found, causes anxiety and hostility and thus an unwillingness to co-operate with new
developments. At this personal impact level the significance of many developments is
not acknowledged as positive action. How many times have you already heard teachers
complain about social workers and the health authority or vice versa? Training and
inspection systems will 'encourage' this way of working, but what other factors need to
be considered if this is to be genuinely achieved, whilst keeping the children's needs at
the heart of all issues?

What?

What will need to be recognised, considered and actioned to enable the changes in working practices required?

If you observe SENCOs or SEN teachers who work for the majority of their time with children with special educational needs many are already very familiar with working with professionals from other statutory agencies. They have established good liaisons, trusting and co-operative relationships, self-confidence, effective communication skills and professional expertise. They recognise that inter-agency working is the only effective way of providing the best education and care for many children and actively seek joint working plans. How has their anxiety and hostility been overcome? What skills do they possess that could be transferred to all their colleagues?

Personal response

There are a number of significant words and phrases that have been included in the sections above that will help you consider the following question. Before reading the question below reread the sections above and identify the aspects that you feel may alter professionals' perceptions of themselves and of their professional ability and standing.

Identify *four* words which illustrate the reasons why you think some teachers may find it challenging to be able to function confidently within an inter-agency framework. Reflect and critically evaluate your selection.

Practical implications and activities

1. With a colleague, examine and explore the following four words I have thought to be of particular relevance:
   - trust;
   - communication;
   - co-operation;
   - self-confidence.

   These four words have been chosen because they pay particular regard to the feelings and views that an individual, building a relationship with an acquaintance, could well be looking for if they want to form a friendship. Do you think you would look for different criteria when working with a professional from another agency, or not? Do you look for different attributes when building a professional relationship with another teacher? Consider critically how you think these criteria may influence whether genuine, focused inter-agency working is effective for the 'clients', in this case the children, and also for teachers.

2. In your opinion what does enable effective inter-agency working?

3. What factors could be detrimental to successful professional partnerships?

4. Are there any aspects of inter-agency working that you would find challenging, as a trainee teacher, and how will you overcome these challenges? Discuss and debate with a friend who is not a trainee teacher/teacher.

Further reading

Blamires, M and Moore, J (2003) *Support services and mainstream schools: a guide for working together*. London: David Fulton.

DfES, (2001b) *Special educational needs code of practice*, Chapter 10, 10:1–10:40, pp135–142. Annesley: DfES.

Roaf, C (2002) *Coordinating services for included children: joined up action*. Buckingham: Open University Press.

Before you read the next extract prepare yourself by reading:

Constable, D (2002) *Planning and organising the SENCO Year*, pp73–77. London: David Fulton.

Gibson, S and Blandford, S (2005) *Managing special educational needs*, Chapter 6, pp98–112. London: Paul Chapman.

Wall, K (2003) *Special needs and early years*, Chapter 4, pp64–85.

Extract: Parkinson, G (2002) 'Interdisciplinary support for children with epilepsy in mainstream schools', pp175–178, in Farrell, P and Ainscrow, M (eds), *Making special education inclusive*. London: David Fulton.

Roles and responsibilities

In their *Teachers' Guide* (BEA Information sheet 2001), the pivotal role of the teacher in early diagnosis is emphasised:

> The teacher can be a great help in the diagnosis of the type of epilepsy a child may have, through an accurate written description of the seizures. Communication between teachers, parents and doctors cannot be stressed strongly enough. This ... also prevents the child from becoming inhibited or withdrawn, or experiencing unnecessary learning problems.
>
> (British Epilepsy Association 2001)

To have a declared intention in the school's or LEA's policy documentation to 'work together' is not specific enough. Dyson, Lin and Millward (1998) in a national study of inter-agency cooperation for children with SEN in the light of the Code of Practice (DFE 1994) restated the need for close and informed cooperation. However, despite widespread consensus 'joint-working' has proved difficult to sustain in practice and there is a long history of difficulties in this area (Dyson *et al.* 1998). One area of difficulty highlighted related to problems with information access, exchange and avoidance of unnecessary duplication. The potential for this to happen can be seen when looking at the possible number of people involved in the education, care and support of children with epilepsy within a mainstream school environment (see Figure 15.1).

This list does not include contact with other more specialised services such as paediatric neurology, or the liaison required with statutory LEA officers, voluntary agencies or transport providers. All need to be clear about their roles and responsibilities; with whom to liaise (named person); and when to inform others of changes in circumstances, either child-centred or in terms of service delivery. Systems and structures will need to adjust as the child's health and academic needs change and as he or she moves through the educational system from primary to secondary education.

The way to achieve clarity of definition of roles and responsibilities, so avoiding unnecessary duplication of assessment and support, seems to be to build into the system a regular review procedure (already in place in schools but not in all LEAs). This review system should actively set out to monitor the 'cooperative activities in which they are engaged' (Dyson *et al.* 1998), paying particular heed to the balance and emphasis on take-up of service provision and the range of approaches and tasks such services are asked to support.

At local authority level such systems would be useful to ensure:

- greater information exchange between education, social care and health services. Some of the common barriers to this were identified by Law, Lindsay, Peacey, Gascoigne, Soloff, Radford and Band (2000) as being:
  a) lack of common boundaries between agencies;
  b) lack of common shared record keeping on children;
  c) difficulties in definitions of posts with consequent recruitment and retention problems (in relation to Speech and Language Therapists (SLTs) in this instance);
- greater recognition of the needs of people with epilepsy and therefore a need for
- a coordinated programme of awareness-raising and training for teaching and allied staffs; plus
- production of clear policy guidelines (jointly devised) for schools in support of students with epilepsy and their families.

At school level the needs were similar with the emphasis on additional training for designated members of staff being required.

In some schools it is generally recognised that there are difficulties and time delays in inter-agency information dissemination and exchange. Mainstream schools are, with the increasing knowledge base and roles of SENCOs, now more likely to know how and what services to access to assist the range of needs they are asked to support when associated with the child with epilepsy. Examples of such service 'definitions' are named contacts in their local Social Services Department (SSD) or Speech and Language Therapy Service (SLT Service). 'Border' disputes over who will pay for SLT Services are particularly common

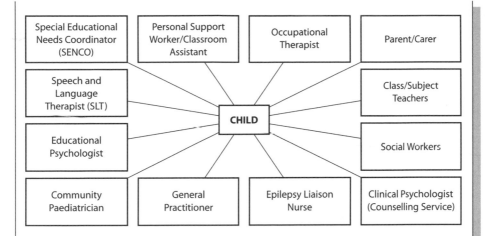

Figure 15.1 Support system for a child with epilepsy

in mainstream schools, where historically health services have only had to provide overtly medical supervision to meet local health needs. Therefore, the concept of using 'defined' service access is a particularly useful one in such circumstance,. The framework for fragmented statutory assessment and review has helped to improve the somewhat fragmented network of service need with their differing organisational frameworks, definitions of need and priorities regarding service delivery.

However, examples of good practice in lines of support are being set up. Clear lines of communication are being created as people become involved and, indeed, the agencies themselves become more informed about the nature of epilepsy, its management, treatment and implications for increased inclusion in schools. One can see from Figure 15.2 how good lines of contact have been established between the SENCO or designated support worker, parents, head of year/head teacher and other agencies.

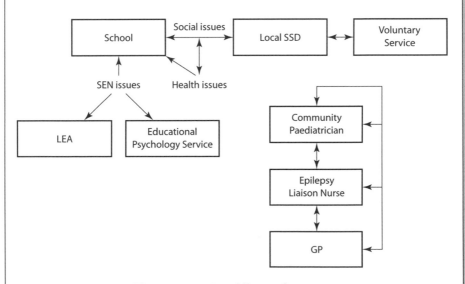

Figure 15.2 Good lines of contact

At a strategic level, an increased number of LEAS, Primary Care Groups (PCGs) and SSDs have improved their lines of communication with the advent of statutory assessments which consider the educational as well as the health needs of children with epilepsy. Gradually service delivery is striving towards the ideal of seamless support and provision. While this is far from a reality in many parts of the UK, the introduction of person-centred or joint action planning for individuals is becoming more evident within local authority and school provision. Descriptions of models of cooperation which are found to be working are in a DfEE report entitled 'Effective Communication between Schools, LEAs and Health and Social Services in the Field of Special Educational Needs' (Dyson *et al.* 1998).

Why?

Why could this 'seamless' service (DfES, 2001b, p135) have to be a long-term aim of the government?

The extract above identifies some positives and also difficulties experienced with inter-agency working in practical situations. Areas of particular problems highlighted by Parkinson (2002) are related to the manner in which agencies collect, record and are able to share information about children. The ability of agencies, including voluntary groups, to exchange and avoid duplication of information can be a problem. Additionally particular issues surround all health information because of the rights of each individual to have their medical history remain private and confidential. To help you consider the significance of these and similar issues think about how you or a teacher you have worked with, write assessment reports or perhaps an Individual Education Plan (IEP) detailing the strengths and weaknesses of children with special educational needs. Could another professional from another agency access the full meaning of the report and the significance of the findings without a good understanding of the current curriculum, educational acronyms and assessment procedures of your school, let alone your attempts to maintain a positive approach? Take another look at Figure 15.1 in the extract. Think of how even a few misunderstandings of terms used or the lack of knowledge about curriculum levels of need, etc, multiplied within this group of professionals could lead to inaccuracies when providing for a child's needs.

This clearly is not an issue that can be dealt with overnight, but will only evolve after methods of working and the various roles and responsibilities of all the support services are fully understood and respected by each other. As the SEN Code of Practice (DfES, 2001b:10:5, p135) says: *Consultative responsibilities and effective communication systems at management and practitioner levels should be clearly identified. Developments in organisational structures and working practices should reflect this principle.*

Opportunities to meet face to face are therefore essential if a true picture of a child's special educational needs are going to be fully understood by all involved. This in itself can create problems because in reality time and the ability of the right staff member being able to attend meetings is not always possible. Perhaps five years ago the SENCO from the school would always attend the joint working meetings regarding children in the school and feedback to the class teacher. The inclusion agenda, however, means that frequently it is the class teacher that should really be part of this inter-agency group, as the child's education is his/her responsibility, but again time and SEN expertise can at present reduce the effectiveness of this approach. For this aspect to improve and for all staff to be fully skilled training will be vital.

How?

How can the government's agenda be taken forward currently as the systems to support the aim are being developed?

It is anticipated that the introduction of the integrated inspection framework will *secure genuine integration of local authority services under the new Director of Children's Services, and (to) encourage a quicker move to Trusts bringing together health and other services* (HMSO, 2003, 5:40, p77). The government has recognised the need for a *common use of language about SEN and disabilities that will enable professionals to improve the way they respond to the needs of children with special educational needs and disabilities and their families* (DfES, 2004, 4.24, p83) as well, but as yet has not stated how this is going to be achieved. They have also responded to the problems that could ensue about various agencies working together without 'a chair' by introducing the role of a designated 'lead professional' who would be responsible for co-ordinating service provision. This lead professional among other responsibilities, the government suggests could act as the 'gatekeeper' for information sharing systems. Other professionals could have partial access but only the lead professional would be aware of the detail. It could be the lead professional who would make a judgement about whether, taken together, the early warnings logged by different practitioners merited intervention (HMSO, 2003, 4.22, 60). How beneficial do you think having a lead professional system will be in enabling an integrated provision that *improves co-ordinated planning and delivery of services* (DfES, 2004, 4.24,83) for children with special educational needs?

Personal response

What are your feelings, as a trainee teacher, about the integration of education, health and social care services around the needs of children? How do you think *extended schools – acting as the hub for services for children, families and other members of the community* (HMSO, 2003,p29) will influence your expectations of teaching in the twenty-first century?

Practical implications and activities

1. What strengths and weaknesses can you identify in the government's plans to develop inter-agency professional working practices? To help you get started read through the following sections in *Every child matters* (2003) and *Removing barriers to achievement – The government's strategy for SEN* (2004) and examine in detail how effective you think each suggestion would be for providing an integrated service for children with special educational needs. Map your views on to a table similar to the one below and then compare this with one completed by a colleague.

	Strengths	Weaknesses
Every child matters (HMSO, 2003)		
Section 18, page 10		
Section 4.8, pages 55–56		
Sections 4.13–4.17		
Sections 4.18–4.22		
Sections 4.23–4.27		
Sections 5.7–5.14		

	Strengths	Weaknesses
Removing barriers to achievement (DfES, 2004)		
Page 72		
Page 73		
Page 82, 4.21		
Page 82, 4.22		
Page 83, 4.24		
Page 86, 4.25–4.31		

Now critically evaluate your answers with your partner colleague. How have these discussions helped you think about skills you are developing for working within an inter-professional environment responsible for ensuring that children with special educational needs are provided with an effective, integrated education and care plan? Consider the following areas:

- identification;
- assessment;

- observation;
- planning;
- reporting;
- evaluating achievement;
- evaluating the appropriateness of provision and strategies utilised.

Further reading

DfES, (2001b) *SEN toolkit*, Sections 11 and 12. Annesley: DfES.

Garner, P and Davies, J (2001) *Introducing special educational needs – a guide for students*. London: David Fulton.

Headington, R (2000) *Monitoring, assessment, recording, reporting and accountability – meeting the standards*. London: David Fulton.

Soan, S (2004) (ed) *Additional educational needs – inclusive approaches to teaching*. Chapter 2, pp13–31. London: David Fulton.

7 Working effectively with colleagues

By the end of this chapter you should have explored and critically evaluated:

- **why** working effectively with colleagues can be, simultaneously, one of the most rewarding aspects of the teaching role, but also one of the most problematic areas within your daily practice, especially when dealing with issues around special educational needs;
- **what** effective collaboration within the school community really means and *how* this varies depending on the different roles of the personnel;
- **how** you can use underpinning theory and literature to support your development and skills in this area.

Linking your learning
Achieving QTS: Professional studies primary phase, second edition, Jacques, K and Hyland, R (2003) Chapter 12.

Professional Standards for QTS
1.5, 1.6, 2.6, 3.1.4, 3.3.13

Introduction

The most significant Professional Standard for this chapter is without question within the 'Teaching and class management' section (3.3). Reference 3.3.13 says that to gain your QTS you must demonstrate that you can *work collaboratively with specialist teachers and other colleagues and, with the help of an experienced teacher as appropriate, manage the working of teaching assistants or other adults to enhance pupils' learning* (Jacques and Hyland, 2003, p204). By separating teaching assistants and other adults from 'colleagues' even the Standards are forewarning you that different skills are likely to be required when working with HLTAs, TAs and other support staff to those needed when working with other teachers. It is vital that, when working with children with special educational needs, the quality of the collaboration between professionals ensures that everyone's expectations of the children, and their understanding of their difficulties and strengths are the same. This means that as a trainee teacher you need to gather the knowledge, understanding and skills to be able to work in this way. I cannot state strongly enough the importance of effective collaborative working partnerships with your colleagues. It can also be far more difficult to achieve on occasions than working with external personnel as discussed in the previous two chapters. This chapter will identify factors that influence effective working partnerships in schools and enable you to assess the impact these will have on how you consciously decide to develop your professional relationships and daily working practices, particularly when focusing on children with special educational needs.

In past years many teachers did not see educating and planning specifically and individually for children with special educational needs as falling within their remit and were quite happy to hand over much of the responsibility of educating children in their mainstream classrooms to the SENCO. This type of approach had a 'knock on effect' on how the classroom teacher would manage the teaching assistants. It also meant that the need for collaboration between specialists, teacher, teaching assistant and the remedial teacher/SENCO was quite limited. However, the introduction of the revised *Special Educational Needs Code of Practice* (DfES, 2001b, 5:2, p44) made it extremely clear that: *All teachers are teachers of children with special educational needs. Teaching these children is therefore a whole school responsibility. In practice, the way in which this responsibility is exercised by individual staff is a matter for schools, to be decided in the light of a school's circumstances and size, priorities and ethos.*

The publication of *Removing barriers to achievement* (DfES, 2004) the government's statutory framework for children with special educational needs refinements took individual teachers responsibilities even further: *All teachers should expect to teach children with special educational needs (SEN) and all schools should play their part in educating children from their local community, whatever their background or ability* (DfES, 2004, Introduction). The government is aware of the immense effect their inclusion agenda is having on schools and teachers and is attempting to use legislation and guidance to support this change. Nevertheless there are issues – such as how schools encourage collaborative working between staff for children with special educational needs, and the training and time required for this – that may in the end determine outcomes.

Before you read the following extract, prepare yourself by reading:

- Croll, P and Moses, D (2000) 'Ideologies and utopias: education professionals' views of inclusion'. *European Journal of Special Needs Education*, 15(1): 1–12.
- Gross, J and White, A (2003) *Special educational needs and school improvement – practical strategies for raising standards*. London: David Fulton.
- HMSO (2003) *Every child matters, 6.9–6.12:86*. Norwich: The Stationery Office.
- TTA (1999) *National special educational needs specialist standards*. London: TTA.
- Weatherley, RA and Lipsky, M (1977) Street-level bureaucrats, p47–50, in Thomas, G and Vaughan, M (2004) (eds), *Inclusive education – readings and reflections*. Maidenhead: OUP.

Extract: HMSO (2003) *Every child matters,* **2.20 and 2.21: 29. Norwich: The Stationery Office.**

Integrating services through extended schools and clusters of schools

2.20 The Government wants to integrate education, health and social care services around the needs of children. To achieve this, we want all schools to become extended schools acting as the hub for services for children, families and other members of the community. Extended schools offer the community and their pupils a range of services (such as childcare, adult learning, health and community facilities) that go beyond their core educational function.

2.21 The Government is also creating a network of full service extended schools, with at least one in every LEA in England by 2006. Each full service school will offer a core of childcare, study support, family and lifelong learning, health and social care, parenting support, sports and arts facilities, and access to Information Technology. By 2006, all LEAs will also be funded to employ school based managers or LEA co-ordinators to develop more services for children and to be provided in school buildings.

Why?

Why is collaborative working considered an aspect of school culture that needs to be fostered and enhanced?

As in the previous chapters of this section the needs, views and beliefs of individual teachers can be very significant when trying to engender new practices. Not all teachers feel they can or want to be teachers of children with special educational needs, despite legislation and guidance telling them they have to be, and this perspective can be deep seated and be based on firmly-held views about education and why they entered the teaching profession originally. In such cases collaboration and whole school co-operation is imperative.

Collaborative working can actually break down previously strongly upheld barriers to the way teachers plan, assess, interact and actually teach children. With positive support from peers, without stigma or concern about not being 'satisfactory', learning, social and behavioural issues can be dealt with, raising the expertise of the teacher as well as the attainment and achievement of the children. If mastered as part of a whole staff culture this will enable an openness of working that will then promote and generate collaborative working, stimulating and broadening staff experience, knowledge and understanding in an informal, but very influential manner. In this way a child with a problem can become the centre of focus without professional issues being a concern, as is evidenced below:

> There is a culture of open co-operation in the school. Every morning, the staff team meet before school starts in order to go through the key events of the day and to share any particular issues or problems. There is no stigma attached to being unable to cope with a child who is behaving in a way which is disruptive to the class. ... It's always been a culture of this school that you don't take on someone's behaviour as your problem. It's a whole school problem and the whole school has to work at it.

and:

> Our SENCO has regular meetings for all children . . . And we share our IEPs and our different ways of doing them. Teachers feel less threatened when they share problems.
>
> (Corbett, 2001, p56)

In such an environment the needs of all pupils become of importance to all the school staff and the involvement of teachers in all aspects of planning and policy becomes the norm. This therefore enables the 'different' and 'extra' requirements for children with special educational needs to become just a normal part of a teacher's daily working role. They know that if additional advice is required this can be asked for and assistance provided in a supportive, co-operative way.

In the future this may even be available from a variety of professionals working together within the school community. Joint decisions, common and consistent practices and approaches towards behaviour and attendance, for example, therefore become accepted by practitioners across the school. This without question provides children with a confidence and security in what is expected of them throughout the school and therefore engenders trust and co-operation from them towards the school and the staff. You can see therefore how collaborative working can foster both positive staff development and trust in each other as professionals and also raise the expectations of all the children. Alongside this the children receive an education where they are valued and taught as individuals in an environment that maintains consistent rules and boundaries.

How?

How will the development of the integration of services through extended schools influence collaborative working with colleagues for teachers?

An extended school will involve a vast move away from the traditional environment teachers have been used to working in. First, the number of colleagues a teacher will be co-operating with on a daily basis is likely to increase. As a new teacher entering the profession, understanding the reasoning and aims behind such a move will clearly give you a positive outlook, but how will it feel at the ground level every day? Teachers are in some cases still trying to adapt their mind-sets to an inclusive agenda and to be effective teachers of all children, especially those with a number of individual differences. Will this put too much pressure on schools and most significantly teachers too soon or not?

The culture of a school will undoubtedly determine how positively it adopts such new practices and this in itself is a prime factor in how far collaborative working is successful. If this is the case will the presence of other professionals and support staff on the school site actually encourage collaboration and thus inclusion? Could collaborative practice actually be an important key to the success of this initiative, steadily moving the agenda along taking all the professionals forward at a speed they can cope with and sustain in practice?

What?

What types of collaborative relationships are there in a school and what skills do they involve?

In a school at the current time you will have to be able to collaborate with many different colleagues carrying out many different roles and having a range of responsibilities.

They will probably involve a number of different staff members and they all will require you to think carefully about how you need to work with them so you can both support the children in your class as successfully as possible. This is also likely to increase and so spending time considering the skills and abilities needed to establish and maintain such a diversity of working relationships will be invaluable.

Clearly you will not require the same amount of liaison or expect the same amount of expertise from the caretaker and, for example, teaching assistants. However, there are a few basic considerations to make when working in such a diverse community to ensure that the whole system you are part of functions efficiently. It is always important to recognise that to work well everyday, all jobs and hence the workers within a community, need to function using the same 'ethos' or 'culture' criteria. Thus, for example, when you need to go and speak to a lunchtime supervisor about making sure a certain child with Autistic Spectrum Disorder does not have to queue for lunch, they will respond positively knowing that although they might not fully understand the reasoning behind this request, the decision would have been made in consultation with colleagues and with the interest of the individual pupil, the adults and the other pupils in mind.

Also as a young teacher I was told that whatever I did, I must not upset the secretary and having the caretaker as a friend was extremely beneficial. What the more experienced staff were passing on to me was that although the caretaker and the secretary did not actually teach the children, their roles and their co-operation was vital to the well-being of the school and hence the teachers and the children. Nevertheless the relationship, level of trust and educational involvement is very different and knowing what and what not to share with personnel in these positions is important.

You may find collaborating with and managing teaching assistants, support staff and perhaps HLTAs quite intimidating to start with, but as the teacher you are the professional responsible for educating the children. With this in mind the working relationship and the collaboration must reflect this fact. You are the professional who, when an inspector visits, must know what each child is doing, whatever their level of need and be able to state how this work fits in with raising their achievement level. However, this does not mean that you do not have a mutual respect for each others roles, and collaboration is vital if assessment and monitoring is going to be successfully achieved for each child.

When collaborating with teaching colleagues there are the opportunities to really seek advice, discuss concerns and strategies attempted, as well as issues such as how best to deal with more challenging behaviour or the head lice problem in the class. Hence all the roles have the children as their central focus, but one role may concentrate more on their physical well-being and another on their social care; your role as a teacher requires you to have an overview of all these aspects with your main focus being their education. A school is therefore not a place to work in if you do not like communicating with adults as well as children. It also requires a high level of social awareness and adaptability.

Personal response

The practical myth ignores the fact that meeting special needs within mainstream schools involves, first and foremost, crucial questions and decisions concerning values and attitudes, rather than 'how' questions related to the curriculum, teaching methods etc. When staff attitudes, values and school ethos are consistent with meeting a wide range of individual needs, the necessary curriculum and organisational reforms will usually follow.

(Dessent,1987–88, in Thomas and Vaughan, 2004, p78)

Reflect on whether, as a trainee teacher, you agree with the statements above. What is Dessent really saying here? Draw a mind map using information from the commentary in the sections above to identify what the major factors are in your view that enhance collaborative working practices and as a consequence also enhances teachers' skills in mainstream schools to effectively teach children with special educational needs.

Practical implications and activities

With a colleague, or two if possible, think of a situation in which a teaching assistant, working with a child with special educational needs, deals with an issue in a manner that completely contradicts the way the class teacher has been dealing with the child's difficulties. The child has social, emotional and behavioural difficulties and will try to avoid completing tasks by inappropriate behaviour. Clearly up to this point there has been little collaboration between the teacher and the teaching assistant.

What does this tell the child about the way in which the teacher and the teaching assistant work?

How would you go about holding a meeting with a teaching assistant if you found yourself in a similar situation? With one of the colleagues acting as an observer (if there are two colleagues) try and act out this meeting as a role play. If able, take turns being the teaching assistant and the teacher. Thinking carefully and critically, evaluate how you felt during each meeting, focusing on:

- what made the meeting productive?
- what were the positive aspects/comments that you could see would lead to collaborative working in the classroom?
- what did you learn not to repeat in another similar meeting?

Engage with what would happen if the same child met with a consistent message from the teaching assistant and the teacher. How would this help:

- the child;
- the teacher;
- the teaching assistant;
- the other children in the class?

Further reading

Booth, T and Ainscow, M (2002), *Index for inclusion*, part 3, A.1.3, A.2.2, A.2.4, A.2.5. Bristol: CSIE.

Dessent, T (1987–8) 'Making the ordinary school special', pp77–83, in Thomas, G and Vaughan, M (2004) *Inclusive Education – readings and reflections*. Maidenhead: OUP.

DfES, (2001a) *Inclusive schooling*. Annesley: DfES.

Before you read the next extract prepare yourself by reading:

- DfES (2004) *Removing barriers to achievement – the government's strategy for SEN*, 3.9–3.15: 56–59. Annesley: DfES.
- TTA, (1998) *National Standards for Special Educational Needs Co-ordinators*. London: TTA.

Extract: Cowne, E (1998) (2nd edn) *The SENCO handbook – working with a whole-school approach*, p82, sections 'Supporting colleagues' and 'The SENCO's role in supporting in-service training for SEN'. London: David Fulton.

Supporting colleagues

Much of what has been said in the previous sections applies to working successfully with colleagues. They too need someone to share concerns, so listening skills will apply here as will problem solving strategies. Often colleagues only need to be reassured that they are doing the right thing. Being able to describe their problem, express their concerns and anxieties will be sufficient to produce the feeling of being supported. It may be wise to follow this up by observation of the child or group in question. Fuller assessment may be part of the solution. Interview with pupil and parents may be indicated.

It is not the SENCOs' role to know all answers to all questions. What they can do is to facilitate the *problem-solving abilities* of their colleagues and help them find solutions which they feel will work. These solutions may require the SENCO to work collaboratively with the class or child, or they may be to request precise advice on strategies or resources. Being able to enter into productive dialogues with colleagues is *the skill* the SENCO will need to develop most. It is, of course, more likely that SENCOs will also have knowledge of a particular strategy or resource to help a particular child, if they have experience of a wide range of SEN themselves or have access to specialist advice (see Chapters 6 and 7).

The SENCO's role in supporting in-service training for SEN
Code of Practice Schedule 1: 13

> *The school's policy should, in accordance with the Code of Practice, describe plans for the in-service training and professional development of staff. Where appropriate, the school's in-service training policy should cover the needs of non-teaching assistants. In drawing up their policies, the school should inform itself of the LEA's in-service training policy and consider both the training needs of the SEN co-ordinator and how he or she can be equipped to provide training for fellow teachers. The school's policy should also set out any joint arrangements with other schools. (Circular 6/94 Par 50)*

It is often seen as central to the SENCO's role to take the lead in in-service sessions on the various aspects of SEN. Just how feasible this is again depends on the existing knowledge and competence level of the SENCO him/herself. Many aspects of SEN policy and procedures can be dealt with in-house by the SENCO. It needs to be recognised, however, that the more specialist areas may not be known by anyone in one school and it is then that help needs to be brought in from outside services or professionals. SENCOs may also wish to set up information corners in the staff room and provide all staff with a folder. This could include guidance on the Code's stages and key information about pupils on the SEN register (see also Chapter 6).

How?

How will learning about the skills a SENCO requires help you as a class teacher learn to collaborate effectively with other colleagues?

Collaboration is an essential skill for a successful SENCO. Without this they will be ineffectual in their role supporting the children with special educational needs, colleagues and parents/carers. Therefore if you wish to identify how to enhance teamwork/co-operation skills for teachers, there is probably no better place to start. Also many of the aspects highlighted in the *National standards for special educational needs co-ordinators* (TTA, 1998) can now be considered part of the role of a class teacher within the inclusion agenda with regard to the teaching and learning of children with special educational needs.

To collaborate successfully with colleagues Cowne (1998, p82) says that SENCOs need to develop excellent listening skills and to participate productively in dialogue. These are skills that will be invaluable for you as a teacher working in an environment such as an extended school where there are a number of colleagues and personnel from outside the usual school community. To be able to listen and to participate in useful discussions you need to be confident, enthusiastic, reliable, flexible and a good communicator, all of which are stated as attributes a SENCO needs (TTA, 1998, p10).

Part of successful collaboration is of course for colleagues to learn from each other, either in formal situations such as INSET or staff meetings, or during meetings about an individual child where additional strategies or methods of teaching previously untried by one of the teachers can be described to them and then utilised in the classroom. Collaboration therefore can be an excellent and efficient method of training teachers in a supportive environment. More recent guidance from the Department for Education and Skills (2004a: 32) *Primary National Strategy – learning and teaching for children with special educational needs in the primary years*, informs class teachers how to ensure that additional adults in the classroom actually improves children's learning. It states that while the key is teamwork, it is important that the class teacher retains ownership of the child's learning. There should be strategies in place to:

- reduce the risk of over-dependency;
- consider whether the additional adult support is enabling interaction between the child and his or her peers, or whether it is inadvertently acting as a barrier to such interaction;
- ensure the support does not sometimes embarrass the pupil;
- enable the additional adult to gain sufficient knowledge of the relevant aspect of the subject to promote children's learning;
- ensure that the additional adult understands what the learning objectives mean in terms of learning outcomes.

All of these aspects require collaborative skills to be in place if they are going to be achieved. The important factor here is that additional adults need to be managed and on many occasions taught skills by the class teacher. If there is not an effective collaborative partnership in place it is very difficult indeed to facilitate such developments.

Why?

Why is it essential to be confident in collaborative working as either a trainee and newly qualified teacher?

The following six indicators illustrated within *Removing barriers to achievement* (DfES, 2004, 3.11:57) identify why it is vital you are both confident in being a collaborative partner and also understand the reasoning behind the introduction of this facet of the role of the teacher in the twenty-first century.

Those awarded Qualified Teacher Status must demonstrate that they can:

- understand their responsibilities under the SEN Code of Practice, and know how to seek advice from specialists on less common types of SEN;
- differentiate their teaching to meet the needs of pupils, including those with SEN;
- identify and support pupils who experience behavioural, emotional and social difficulties.

Standards for the Induction Support Programme for those awarded Qualified Teacher Status require:

- the head teacher to ensure that all Newly Qualified Teachers (NQTs) understand the duties and responsibilities schools have under the Disability Discrimination Act 1995 to prevent discrimination against disabled pupils;
- the induction tutor to arrange for NQTs to spend time with the school's SENCO to focus on specific and general SEN matters;
- the NQT to demonstrate that they plan effectively to meet the needs of pupils in their classes with SEN, with or without statements.

No longer is it down to senior managers or SENCOs to be the collaborators – all teachers need to be fully involved in the learning and teaching of all the children in the class whatever their needs. *What* you do to support learning, especially with children with special education needs, is still a part of individualised learning, but it is far more the *why* and *how* you, the class teacher, enable and enhance achievement and learning that is part of the inclusive classroom.

Personal response

Reflect carefully on your professional and social skills already acknowledged during previous teaching practices or in another working environment, that will enable you to participate in effective collaborative work. How do you feel these skills will benefit your teaching, and children's learning within the first one or two years of your career? Critically explore skill areas that you need to develop further and identify avenues to enable you to practise them. Create a plan to enable this work to be achieved prior to entering your first teaching position.

Practical implications and activities

Reread the six indicators listed in the previous section. These combine many of the facets of collaborative partnerships that have been discussed throughout this chapter, although at first glance they are not very obvious. How well do you think you will be able to achieve these indicators without the collaborative support of a colleague, the SENCO or a teaching assistant? In the list below are a number of phrases. How effectively could you action these indicators without teamwork? Write comments into the collaborative section of the table and interrogate your responses carefully.

Indicators	Collaborative?
Understand responsibilities and duties	
Seek advice	
Meet the needs of pupils with SEN	
Identify	
Support	
Spend time with the SENCO	

Describe a school environment in which an NQT would find it difficult to achieve many of these indicators through no fault of his/her own and then examine possible reasons for the government to have included these indicators in the standards.

Further reading

Blandford, S (2005a) *Sonia Blandford's Masterclass*. London: Sage.

DfES, (2004a) *Primary National Strategy – learning and teaching for children with special educational needs in the primary years*. Annesley: DfES.

Disability Rights Commission (2002) *Code of practice for schools – Disability Discrimination Act 1995: Part 4*. London: The Stationery Office.

8 Pupil participation

By the end of this chapter you should have considered and reflected upon:

- **why** it is essential for you to have an underpinning knowledge and understanding of the reasons for ensuring pupil participation is constantly considered and enhanced;
- **what** the practical implications are of improving pupil participation for you as a teacher, the working relationships you form with the pupils and for a school as a whole community;
- **how** you will consult, implement and reflect on your practices to develop pupil participation.

Linking your learning
Achieving QTS: Professional studies primary phase, second edition, Jacques, K and Hyland, R (2003) Chapter 12.

Professional Standards for QTS
1.2, 3.2.2, 3.2.6, 3.2.7, 3.3.1.

Introduction

The voice of the pupil still continues to be a controversial area of discussion. Issues regarding pupils' age and ability are constantly given as reasons for not developing and encouraging pupil participation in the decision-making processes to meet their own educational and social needs. Indeed even Articles 12 and 13 of the United Nations Convention on the Rights of the Child (DfES, 2001:3, Section 4) state:

> Children, who are capable of forming views, have a right to receive and make known information, to express an opinion, and to have that opinion taken into account in any matters affecting them. The views of the child should be given due weight according to the age, maturity and capability of the child.

This clearly does not give you clear guidance about when and how you are to include pupils with special educational needs in decision-making processes. In addition to discussions about the curriculum, behaviour and evaluating progress many pupils with special educational needs may also have to consider issues such as mobility, medical care, outside agency intervention, long-term plans and appropriate placement issues. Pupil participation in many of these incidences has to be individually and carefully considered by all the adults involved. However, not everyone feels it is impossible to create an environment, using child-friendly approaches, that enables pupils to effectively participate in discussions about their own education and future needs. Roaf (2002) and Clough and Barton (1995) clearly illustrate how the voice of the pupil can be heard and listened to so that successful outcomes are achieved.

Indeed pupil participation may be a great matter of concern for you at this stage of your training, because you undoubtedly understand the risks are many if you get this wrong. If you allow pupils to participate in too much and inappropriately you are in danger of undermining your position in a manner that could cause the onset of other issues such as behaviour problems and general classroom control. However, if you do not encourage and support independent thinking and the development of decision-making skills you are also not enabling the pupils to reach their potential and to participate as fully as they are able.

Learning when and how to enable pupil participation is therefore an issue that demands considerable understanding of the pupils you teach and their learning and emotional needs, an openness to collaborate with other colleagues and a willingness to allow the pupils to make final decisions when appropriate. This is therefore an area of daily practice you will need to explore and reflect upon in detail utilising theory, guidance and legislation to inform you about *why* pupil participation is encouraged, *what* the educational and social benefits are and *how* it can enhance your professional practice.

Before you read the following extract, prepare yourself by reading:

- Riddell, S, (2000) 'Inclusion and choice: mutually exclusive principles in special educational needs', pp118–119, in Armstrong, F, Armstrong, D and Barton, L (eds) (2000) *Inclusive education – policy, contexts and comparative perspectives*. London: David Fulton.
- Gibson, S, and Blandford, S (2005) *Managing special educational needs*, pp22–24. London: Paul Chapman.
- DfES, (2001b) *Special Educational Needs Code of Practice*, pp27–31. Annesley: DfES.

Extract: Armstrong, D (1995) *Power and partnership in education*, pp69–71. London: Routledge.

Educational legislation has lagged some way behind the 1989 Children Act. Although some commentators have argued that the 1981 Education Act embodied a radical extension of consumer rights, by creating opportunities for parents to be involved in the assessment of their children's special educational needs, the Act is silent about the contribution of children themselves to the assessment process. The Department of Education and Science (DES 1989a), in its advice on assessments under the 1981 Education Act, nevertheless recommends that 'The feelings and perceptions of the child should be taken into account and the concept of partnership should wherever possible be extended to older children and young persons' (para. 21).

In view of these developments it is perhaps surprising to find that with regard to educational decision-making children remain very much the 'property' of their parents. For instance, the 1988 Education Reform Act implicitly rejects any claim children might have to be consumers of educational services by denying them the right to be consulted over the schools they will attend and the curriculum they will study. Indeed, Rosenbaum and Newell (1991) have argued that it is in respect of the child's role in educational decision-making that the United Nations Charter on the Rights of Children is most seriously disregarded in Britain today.

The 1993 Education Act does, for the first time, establish the principle that the child's views should be sought during an assessment of their special educational needs (Regulation 6). The Code of Practice on the Identification and Assessment of Special Educational Needs (DFE 1994), issued under the 1993 Education Act, has elaborated upon this by identifying the importance of involving children both on grounds of principle – 'children have the right to be heard, therefore should be encouraged to participate in decision-making about provision to meet their special educational needs' – and good practice – 'children have important and relevant information. Their support is crucial to the effective implementation of any individual education programme.' The inclusion of this statement of the importance of the child's role in the assessment has been widely applauded, but these general statements are not unproblematic and indeed may considerably oversimplify the difficulties encountered by professionals in gaining access to children's perspectives. Moreover, they may oversimplify the implications for the child of participation in an assessment.

Gersch, drawing on personal construct theory, has argued that psychological theory provides a strong rationale for giving children a more active role in their own assessments.

> People negotiate the world, interpreting what is experienced, and base their perceptions on their past experiences and anticipations. Within Personal Construct Theory people are seen as active participants and not passive recipients of external events. Each person creates his or her own experiential world, which includes events in the outside world, as well as thoughts, emotions and sensations. Additionally constructions are based upon memories, anticipations, hopes, fears and plans. In short, to understand the person one must understand his or her own construction of the world and the underlying bases of those constructions. Problems can arise when there is a mismatch between the person's own view of events and those of others. It is vital, therefore, to recognize and acknowledge that each person has their own unique and individual interpretation of the world.
>
> (Gersch 1987: 151)

Gersch goes on to discuss four projects on pupil involvement in assessments under the 1981 Education Act in which he has been involved. He argues that the success of these projects (judged on the criterion of the positive responses of pupils participating in them) illustrate that it is possible to increase the active involvement of some children in the assessment process by creating opportunities for the child to express a view of situations even though that view might be in conflict with that of his or her teachers. By adopting such techniques and involving the child, the origins of conflict can be better identified and consensus over the resolution of conflicts more easily obtained.

How?

How has current legislation and national strategy paid regard to Gersch's argument, especially in regard of pupils with special educational needs?

It is undoubtedly recognised that listening and responding to the pupil's voice strengthens the educational provision provided for pupils, giving them a real sense of ownership. As Gersch argues in the extract given above, no one, even the parents or carers understands a pupil better than the pupil him/herself. However, I remember very clearly how decisions about educational interventions and provision for pupils with special educational needs have been made without any consideration at all for what the individual pupil actually wants. This surely must be as inappropriate as a case I heard about when a young adult with severe communication needs, on being given training and support to use symbols for the first time actually managed to use symbols to say, 'no thank you. I hate gravy on my Sunday dinner'. He had been given gravy every Sunday since he moved to the establishment a number of years before!

Legislation and guidance since 1995 has altered quite significantly to support and enable educators to evaluate and reflect on when and how pupil participation is valuable and not burdensome to the child. *Every child matters* (HMSO, 2003) mentions the need for involving children in developments, but it is not a factor highlighted in *Removing barriers to achievement* (DfES, 2004). However, the *Special Educational Needs Code of Practice* (2001) is one guidance document that reflects current thinking about including pupils as fully as possible in decision-making processes. The SEN Toolkit (2001c) booklet entitled *Enabling pupil participation*, will support you as a trainee teacher in considering ways that you can and should enable pupils' views and feelings to be an equal voice in learning processes. It is also not just a once termly 'add-on', but 'must be meaningful and ongoing for all pupils' (DfES, 2001c, *SEN Toolkit booklet* 3, p3).

As a practitioner you will need to explore ways that you can enable and include pupils with special educational needs in daily classroom issues and decisions, as well as in their own educational and social needs. This strategy is seen as sometimes problematic for these pupils, but the government in the *Primary National Strategy – Learning and teaching for children with special educational needs in the primary years* (DfES, 2004, p18) informs you that there are four key areas to ensure you are developing, that will enable pupil participation. The key areas suggested are:

- having a voice and being listened to;
- being active participants in their own learning;
- collaborating with and supporting peers;
- engaging with the local and wider community.

This guidance continues *The ideas that have been generated to develop pupil participation, so as to improve relationships, behaviour, attendance and achievement* (p18). However, although I do not dispute the statement that the key areas identified would facilitate the improvements highlighted, I believe that teachers who form positive relationships with their pupils with special educational needs, have an effective behaviour strategy and also have appropriately high expectations of them, will within their daily practice already be valuing and encouraging pupil participation. It is indeed the special times when a pupil knows he/she has succeeded in a task and how he/she has achieved it that makes teaching pupils with special educational needs so rewarding.

Why?

Why is there the need to establish and expand pupil participation in the classroom for pupils with special educational needs?

Consider and examine the situations in which you learn best. Think back to the times you have been told by a teacher that obviously does not even know your name let alone your individual needs as a learner, to complete a task that appears pointless and you do not even understand. How did you feel? How did you behave and what did you learn? I suspect the answers to the first two questions are varied, but most probably involved negative behaviour or a loss of confidence and self esteem, or both. What did you learn – perhaps how to be an independent thinker and learner – but most probably, and most certainly for those with special educational needs, you would have learnt nothing positive from such an experience. Now reflect on a time when you had a brilliant time in school and really felt you had succeeded. For pupils with special educational needs to play an active role in their learning the teacher will need to:

- understand their individual learning and/or social, emotional and behavioural needs;
- build a positive relationship with the pupils;
- have high, appropriate expectations of pupils with regard to their learning, behaviour and social skills;
- be interested in them as people and as learners;
- listen, observe and be willing to alter your practice to meet the pupils' individual needs;
- encourage opportunities for peer collaboration when teaching learning and social skills;
- involve them in target setting, assessment and evaluation and thus consequently in planning.

Compare these statements with how you felt about your positive experience of learning. Are there any similarities?

What?

What does this tell you about the importance of pupil participation for learners with special educational needs?

And what does it inform you as a trainee teacher about the role confidence, self-esteem and learning relationships have in enabling and enhancing the learning and teaching environment?

Personal response

Examine and critically evaluate the relevance of personal construct theory and statements such as *children and young people with special educational needs have a unique knowledge of their own needs and circumstances and their own views about what sort of help they would like to help them make the most of their education*

(DfES, 2001b, 3:2, p27). Do you agree that planned and well-considered activities/meetings to enable pupil participation, supports the learning and teaching environment? Discuss with a colleague.

Review how pupil participation supports:

- the learner with special educational needs;
- the teacher;
- the other pupils in the (a) class; (b) school;
- other participants including the parents/carers.

Practical implications and activities

Using the *SEN Code of Practice Toolkit*, 3, (DfES, 2001c) to help you, identify five ways you would introduce pupil participation for learners with special educational needs into your classroom. Ensure the ideas are not just 'add-ons' and that they will improve the pupils' whole learning experience and attainment. Ask a colleague to do the same. Reflect on what your answers tell you both about your teaching practice and your belief in the value of pupil participation.

Further reading

Armstrong, D (1995) *Power and partnership in education*. London: Routledge.

DfES (2001b) *Special Educational Needs Code of Practice*, Chapter 3, pp27–31. Annesley: DfES.

DfES (2004) *Primary National Strategy – learning and teaching for children with special educational needs in the primary years*, pp18–23. Annesley: DfES.

Hanam, D (2003) 'Participation and responsible action for all students', in *Teaching citizenship*. (Spring, 2003). Association for Citizenship Teaching.

Before you read the next extract prepare yourself by reading:

- Corbett, J (2001) 'Teaching approaches which support inclusive education: a connective pedagogy'. *British Journal of Special Education*, 2001, Vol. 28(2): 55–59.
- Teaching and Learning Research Programme (2004) *Personalised learning – a commentary by the teaching and learning research programme*. Economic and Social Research Council. **www.tlrp.org**

Look at:
www.nuffieldcurriculumcentre.org (follow links to citizenship)
www.teachernet.gov.uk/pupil

Extract: Cowne, E (1998) *The SENCO handbook – working within a whole-school approach* (2nd edn) pp75–77. London: David Fulton.

Enhancing pupil perspectives

To achieve an understanding of the pupils' own view of their school experience and their educational needs requires an ability on behalf of the teacher to change perspective. Teachers have to let go of their position of authority, for a short time, and view the world of the classroom from the pupils' point of view. This may best be done through becoming a careful observer for certain times and taking very detailed notes. If someone else can manage the class for a short session while this observation takes place, it may be easier to be free to observe.

Observation impartiality

Accurate observation for as little as ten minutes, if focused and prepared, can give some insights into a particular area of concern, whether an individual pupil or a group. Always remember that observation will be affected by bias, so if more than one adult can observe to a prepared schedule, the results may be more reliable.

Observation skills

Learning observation skills gives teachers a useful tool for assessment and general problem solving. Observation can be for set times (e.g. ten minutes) or of specific events or of a specific context, such as the playground. Starting the observation without a precise focus may be possible, but increasingly focusing in on an intended feature may give more insight. If pupil perspectives are the focus, this may need to be combined with interview techniques. There are a number of observation techniques given in Appendix 9a.

Interviews

Another way to get a pupil's perspective is, of course, to ask the pupil to talk about or express their views in some way. This can be by direct questions about an aspect of their work, such as reading or homework, or it can be more open-ended questioning about school, friends, events etc. Open-ended interviewing is difficult for some teachers to do, partly because of time constraints, partly because it is a skill to be learnt. Sometimes other adults, ancillary helpers or support professionals may fare better, because they may offer less threat to pupils, or have time to see pupils in a more relaxed environment.

Questionnaires

The whole class can be given exercises to evaluate an aspect of their own learning, possibly to give ratings about how confident they feel about various aspects of their learning. For younger pupils, faces with different expressions can be used to rate answers instead of words (see Appendix 9b).

Triangulation

It is more difficult to gain a view of pupil perspective where the pupil lacks the language to express their thoughts and feelings in words. In these cases observations from more than one adult may need to be combined to giving a feel for the pupil's perspective. Ancillary helpers' and parents' observations about different aspects of the pupil's development and feelings of self-worth are very helpful in putting together a joint perspective. If video cameras and tape recorders are used, this can help collect valuable data in cases where more direct questioning is difficult, for example, the developmentally young or pupils with language impairment. These would not be kept as a long-term record, but might help analyse complex observations.

Symbolic representation

Drawings and symbolic representations of situations as perceived during play can all add to the teacher's understanding of pupil perspectives.

Learning observation and interview techniques

All of the above takes time, just for one child, and will not be possible to do for all the pupils in a class or on the SEN register. Different methods can be selected for different children and at different times. It is useful however if, as part of training sessions, teachers can practise some of the skills required in collecting and collating information which will enhance their ability to look at pupil perspectives. For some teachers, the exercise of *really* trying to understand one pupil, from a child's point of view, is a revelation (see Appendix 9a and b).

Why?

Why is the intervention or strategy utilised by teachers vital for gaining accurate views of pupils with special educational needs?

Commentary and ideas offered by Cowne (1998) reflect clearly government and professional views at the end of the twentieth century. However, the ideas she suggests Special Educational Needs Co-ordinators (SENCOs) may use to help them understand pupil perspectives can be easily transferable for teachers and support staff in today's classrooms. Corbett (2001), however, takes you from the end of the twentieth to the beginning of the twenty-first century, using her own enquiries as evidence to illustrate how an inclusive school encourages pupil participation for learners with special educational needs. Linking with discussions earlier on in the chapter she says it is: *looking inside out, in order to understand our own responses and the ways in which we, as teachers, can create negative learning situations through unconscious behaviour patterns* (2001, p58) that is vital. The three sentences below demonstrate how Corbett (2001, p58) identifies the importance a school with inclusive approaches values and endorses committed pupil participation, even for learners with special educational needs:

1. When a boy . . . because of his challenging behaviour, asked to go into the adjoining empty room to work on his own with the specialist teacher, this request was complied with. His choice was respected.
2. There is a real effort made to involve the learners, to create situations in which they can meet with success and to build on their existing level of knowledge.
3. They are constantly made aware that they are active participants in the school community and that their views are taken seriously.

There will not be one or even a handful of interventions or strategies that will help you identify every pupil's perspective and encourage their participation, but rather your confidence and *how* far you, as a teacher, are willing to listen and learn from them.

How?

How can you as a trainee teacher begin to identify ways to help pupils with special educational needs participate?

The first most obvious way is to underpin your practice by theory and research evidence. The documentation and literature introduced throughout this chapter will not only have given you a basis on which to start, but importantly will have encouraged you to evaluate critically and reflect on all the information and evidence. If you do this then when you need to put an action into practice you will have the grounding and security to know that your suggestion is based on good evidence and that you have considered factors such as the level of expectations, and learning and social needs.

When in the classroom there are a number of ways you can identify methods of enabling pupils to participate and for their perspective to be listened and responded to. Cowne (1998), Corbett (2001) and government guidance provide illustrations and case studies to examine.

What?

What you do and how successful it is will undoubtedly depend on your willingness and confidence to include the pupils, even those with quite severe needs, to have an input into the curriculum, and the way you manage and teach the class. This is not an easy task, but if achieved in a professional manner, it will benefit the whole learning environment. For example, when you want to introduce a whole class issue such as rules for behaviour why not ask the pupils if they think they are reasonable and whether they would like to write a few rules for you the teacher. Immediately I can hear teachers cry 'they will not take this seriously', but if you clearly show you are genuinely interested in their reasons for particular stipulations they will not only provide good ideas, but will take ownership of the class rules enabling a really collaborative approach towards important issues such as behaviour and respect for others and hence fewer problems for you the teacher.

When tackling individual ways of working with pupils with special educational needs always begin by listening, observing and building a relationship with the pupil. Additional support or training concerning the learning and/or physical need can be sought from either the SENCO or outside providers. It is once again your willingness to criticise or to re-evaluate what you are providing for pupils that will really show your genuine commitment to pupil participation. Teaching, just like learning, should mean you are constantly adjusting and adapting practice to enable you to teach in the most proficient effective manner possible for the pupils who are currently in your class.

Personal response

Examine with a colleague the following statement:

'I cannot teach this pupil. I do not know enough about autism.'

Explore whether you consider this a justified response when a head teacher asks you to welcome this pupil into your class.

- What would you think a reasonable answer would have been?
- What would you seek to do to enable a positive introduction to your class to be achieved for this pupil?
- Once successfully introduced into the class what would you see to be vital you did to enable this pupil to really participate in decision-making about his/her education and how would you initiate this?

If your first thoughts are 'I could not cope' then reflect on why your natural instinct was to respond in this way. Write the reasons down and then on the opposite side of the paper place possible solutions. Now critically evaluate the process you engaged with and whether you would now be more confident to work with a pupil with needs of which you have little prior knowledge and understanding.

Practical implications and activities

1. Which of the following skills do you think are vital for you to develop to enable you to plan, assess and evaluate pupils' learning and participation more effectively?
   - listening;
   - building relationships;
   - consulting;
   - observing;
   - respecting pupils' individual needs and ways of working;
   - learning from the pupils;
   - responding creatively to individual needs to enable access to, engagement with and participation in the curriculum and life of the class and school.

   Using supportive materials such as the *Primary National Strategy* (DfES, 2004a), the *Special Educational Needs Code of Practice* (2001b), the *SEN Toolkit*, booklet 3 (2001c) as well as specifically relevant literature build a small resource bank of ideas and strategies, based on sound theoretical guidance.

2. Work with a colleague to set up a role play situation in which you are the teacher and the other person is the pupil. If the focus skill is to improve listening, then construct a discussion where you would need to really listen to enable an effective response. Record the role play so that you can with your colleague have time to evaluate your responses and reflect on whether you were, for example, genuinely listening to the 'pupil' to enable you to learn and therefore adapt your practice to meet his/her need more appropriately.

Further reading

Byers, R (1999) 'The National Literacy Strategy and pupils with special educational needs'. *British Journal of Special Education*, 26(1): 8–11.

Corbett, J and Norwich, B (1999) 'Learners with special educational needs', in Mortimore, P (ed) *Understanding pedagogy and its impact on learning*. London: Paul Chapman.

DfES, (2004a) *Primary National Strategy – learning and teaching for children with special educational needs in the primary years*. Annesley: DfES.

Mittler, P (2000) *Working towards inclusive education: social contexts*. London: David Fulton.

Norwich, B and Lewis, A (2005) 'How specialized is teaching pupils with disabilities and difficulties?', in Lewis, A and Norwich, B (ed) *Special teaching for special children? – pedagogies for inclusion*. Maidenhead: OUP.

Section 3
Practical Applications in the Primary Classroom

9 The identification and assessment of need

> **By the end of this chapter you should have considered, analysed and reflected upon:**
>
> - **why** identification and assessment is necessary for every child in your class;
> - **what** legislation, documentation and underpinning theory can help you understand the importance of identifying need as early as possible and utilising appropriate assessment to inform practice;
> - **how** identification of need and assessment can inform your planning and methods of teaching, to enable all the pupils in the class to access, engage and participate in learning.
>
> **Linking your learning**
> *Achieving QTS: Professional studies primary phase*, second edition, Jacques, K and Hyland, R (2003) Chapter 12.
>
> **Professional Standards for QTS**
> 3.2.1, 3.2.2, 3.2.3, 3.2.4, 3.2.6, 3.2.7

Introduction

The identification and assessment of need for children with special educational needs can be quite a lengthy and involved process and I have always felt that teachers and especially SENCOs need to be really good detectives, searching out the truth in order to enable learning and teaching to be as effective as possible for all the members of a class. The importance and value of this work under the umbrella of inclusive education is, I believe, far more worthwhile, for adults and children alike, than it was when children with special educational needs were either segregated or integrated.

Before you read the following extract, prepare yourself by reading:

Constable, D (2002) *Planning and organising the SENCO year*. London: David Fulton.

Cowne, E (1998) *The SENCO handbook*. London: David Fulton.

DfES, (2001b) *Special Educational Needs Code of Practice*. Chapter 5, pp44–58, Annesley: DfES.

Farrell, M (2001) *Standards and special educational needs.* pp16–18, London: Continuum.

Wall, K (2003) *Special needs and early years.* Chapter 5, pp86–109, London: Paul Chapman.

Extract: Wedell, K (2000) 'Putting "inclusion" into practice: points from the SENCo-Forum'. *British Journal of Special Education*, 29(3): 151.

Points from the SENCo-Forum

'All teachers should be teachers for special needs' – but is it yet possible?

The policies to promote inclusive education are bringing children and young people with a wider range of special educational needs into mainstream classrooms. A recent message exchange among members of the SENCo-Forum considered how well these children's needs were in fact being met. Two areas of concern were expressed. The first concerned the provision of the necessary expertise to meet pupils' needs. The second concerned the scope that staff in mainstream classrooms had to meet special educational needs.

Participants in the message exchange were concerned about what happened to the pool of staff expertise when special schools or units were closed. In general, it was the case that these staff possessed skills and understanding of the needs of their children. Furthermore, working with other staff in their specialist settings ensured their continued development. Members of the Forum who had moved from special schools and units to mainstream schools felt that, over time, they were losing their specialist competencies. They also felt that the range of general demands placed on them as mainstream teachers made it difficult for them to respond to individual pupils' needs as they had previously done, particularly the emotional and behavioural needs. One message made the point that 'Teachers need to understand where a child is`coming from.' Pupils with these needs were now predominantly those referred for special provision. Are Local Education Authorities in a position to capitalise on and maintain their pool of staff expertise?

SENCos and other staff in mainstream schools felt frustrated at being aware of the individual needs of pupils in their classrooms, and yet unable to respond to them adequately. Some described how they were visited by hard-pressed advisory teachers, who consulted on the formulation of Individual Educational Plans, and then rushed on, leaving the teachers with the problem of carrying out the prescriptions. Some teachers felt that they lacked the training to be aware of the range of pupils' needs. One teacher described how he had been faced with angry parents, who wanted to know why he had not noticed that their child had a particular disability. Certain teachers in the message exchange felt that they did meet the diverse needs of their pupils, but their descriptions showed the amount of time and effort this required. While appreciating the contribution these teachers were making, other messages commented that it was inappropriate for the system to require such demands.

There were comments that the present organisation of schools militated against teachers responding to the individual needs of pupils as effective inclusion demanded. The standard ways in which children were grouped and timetabled hampered the flexibility needed to match the learning needs of pupils at any given time. The content and pace of the National Curriculum was not geared to the particular needs of children with special educational needs and the assessment approaches made it difficult to accord value to the progress children might be making, for example, in their social responsiveness. There was too little recognition that the requirements of effective inclusion were in fact more costly for schools. It was felt that some children were being 'offered as sacrificial lambs on the altar of inclusion'.

None the less, participants in this message exchange were almost unanimously in support of the principles of inclusion. Schools should expect to meet the individual needs of all the children in their catchment areas, so that they could grow up together as members of their community. It was acknowledged that, at present, some children with more severe and specific needs might have to have these met in special schools or units. Even so, there were many ways in which such placements could avoid total segregation from the mainstream through flexible arrangements between settings, in order to maintain optimal contacts.

In contrast to the depressing comments on the limitations of prevailing approaches to mainstream inclusion, there were also accounts of some schools that were nearer to achieving effectiveness. These schools had set their own agenda and established an ethos of valuing individual children as a part of the everyday life of all in the school. The schools were achieving success despite – rather than because of – the education system. Participants listed some of the main features that enabled the schools to improve. These involved implementing communication and collaboration among class teachers, the support staff in and outside the schools, and with staff in the Social and Health Services. Flexible approaches to pupil grouping and timetabling were crucial, including strategic involvement of teaching assistants and collaboration with parents. Pupil peer support was valued. However, it was invariably apparent that these approaches made great demands on individual teachers.

It was clear from the message exchange that the principle of inclusion is widely supported, but the education system as it is experienced is frequently frustrating rather than facilitating its implementation. There is concern that the special educational needs of children are not being adequately met. The recent legislative aspirations to meet the individual needs of all pupils will have to take account of those aspects of the system that militate against inclusion.

Klaus Wedell on behalf of the BECTA special needs team: Chris Stevens (manager) and Terry Waller (projects officer).

Further details about the Forum and how to join are available from **Jason_Douglas@becta.org.uk** or from the Special Needs Administrator, BECTA, Milburn Hill Road, Science Park, Coventry CV4 7JJ. Tel: 02476 416994; Fax: 02476 411418.

Why?

Why are current methods and thinking behind the identification and assessment of need for children with special educational needs considered more beneficial?

The first most important reason is that identification and assessment currently takes place in order to positively inform classroom practice, to enable teachers to understand the learning and environmental needs of children with special educational needs. Prior to the agenda for inclusive education the identification and assessment of need was mostly carried out so that a child could be labelled and then have human and material resources 'attached' to him or her. It was definitely part of the deficit medical model and was sometimes used to remove children from mainstream placements into special schooling. Therefore neither identification or assessment of need was regularly used by teachers as a way of informing their practice or planning in the normal classroom.

Second, assessments are now focused on identifying particular needs and are far more vigorously selected and carried out on a need-to-know basis. Parents, pupils, outside agencies, as well as school staff, are all involved in identifying the reasons for assessment and the information hoped for as a result of the assessment(s). In fact, as one teacher wrote: *teachers need to understand where a child is coming from* (Wedell, 2000, p151). They need to know so that they can then use strategies and teaching styles in a way that will engage as many pupils as possible, encouraging motivation, self-esteem and actually enhancing learning. For those that require additional and different support, it can be managed by the class teacher in a manner that will still enable the children to feel part of the class and very much involved in learning. You will, with the support of more experienced staff within your school, have to develop your skills and knowledge of the different kinds of need and of appropriate assessments to be able to support all of the children in this way.

I do not intend to discuss assessments specifically for statutory purposes. Although class teachers are fully involved in this process, if it is required for an individual pupil, the actual bureaucratic and assessment aspects are dealt with by the SENCO. Hence my intention is to deliberate on the children that may need School Action or School Action Plus support within their mainstream environment.

How?

How has legislation and guidance influenced change and informed practice to improve teachers ability to identify need?

The revised *Special Educational Needs Code of Practice* (DfES, 2001b, p46) high-lighted the need for early identification and for ongoing assessment, looking at all aspects of a child's development as well as learning:

> The importance of early identification, assessment and provision for any child who may have special educational needs cannot be over-emphasised. The earlier action is taken, the more responsive the child is likely to be, and the more readily can intervention be made without undue disruption to the organisation of the school. Assessment should not be regarded as a single event, but rather as a continuing process.

Included in this document are also suggested measures by which to assess individual's progress, but these are broad and class teachers may well require additional support to utilise them.

There are four areas of need identified within the *Special Educational Needs Code of Practice* (DfES, 2001b, p85) following the medical model initiated by the Warnock Report (DES,1978):

- communication and interaction;
- cognition and learning;
- behaviour, emotional and social development;
- sensory and/or physical.

You may find that these four areas can be helpful when initially trying to identify a need; as long as you do not attempt to align a child's need totally within the fixed boundaries of one area. However, the Code (DfES, 2001b, p85) does also state that:

this guidance does not assume that there are hard and fast categories of special educational need. It recognises that ... each child is unique.

Recognising the importance of early identification the government SEN Strategy, *Removing barriers to achievement* (DfES, 2004, p9) starts its first chapter with:

Early identification is the cornerstone of our strategy. Every child matters recognised the lasting benefits of early intervention – providing a sound foundation for future learning and development. It enables some children to catch up with their classmates and for those who need support on a continuing basis it means that help is available as early as possible, reducing the risk of long-term underachievement and disaffection.

What?

What does assessment actually mean and how can it improve learning?

Assessment as discussed earlier has also evolved into a collaborative, proactive action. The *Primary National Strategy – learning and teaching for children with special educational needs in the primary years*, (DfES, 2004a, p13) guidance says:

Assessment for learning is the process of seeking and interpreting evidence for use by learners and their teachers to decide where the learners are in their learning, where they need to go and how best to get there.

To help you further, it also provides five factors the DfES (2004a, p13) states that research has found improves learning through assessment. These are:

- providing effective feedback to pupils;
- actively involving pupils in their own learning;
- adjusting teaching to take account of the results of assessment;

- recognising the profound influence assessment has on the motivation and self-esteem of pupils, both of which are crucial to learning;
- considering the need for pupils to be able to assess themselves and to understand how to improve.

Additionally, the DfES states that effective assessment for children with special educational needs should be based on developing:

- designing learning opportunities – planning;
- using the context of whole-school curricular targets;
- effective strategies for day-to-day assessment;
- feedback on learning;
- involving parents and carers;
- formative use of summative assessment to inform and involve learners.

Personal response

1. Critically consider if and why you feel it is necessary to identify and assess the needs of children with special educational needs.
2. What classroom indicators will inform you that a child may be experiencing learning difficulties? Write these down and then reflect on how (a) you could have prevented a child experiencing these problems and (b) how you facilitate assessment and intervention to support and improve this child's (and possibly others) learning.
3. If assessment is a process and not a static statement how do you envisage it will influence your professional practice and hence your attitude towards teaching children with special educational needs?

Practical implications and activities

A teacher cannot be expected to know everything about special educational needs. However, they are expected to be able to identify a problem and to seek additional support and advice from colleagues, parents, LEA advisers and other agencies in order to help the child overcome the barriers to their learning. Consider the processes that you will need to develop in order to identify and assess children with various difficulties within your classroom. Debate with a colleague:

- what skills and understanding you will need to establish;
- how you will construct and plan various forms of identification and assessment;
- who you will go to for guidance and additional expertise.

Further reading

Blandford, S (2005) *Remodelling schools: workforce reform*. London: Pearson.

Golder, G, Norwich, B and Bayliss, P (2005) 'Preparing teachers to teach pupils with special educational needs in more inclusive schools: evaluating a PGCE development'. *British Journal of Special Education* (32)2: pp92–99.

Horsfall, B (2004) 'Special educational needs and the teacher', in Jacques, K and Hyland, R, *Achieving QTS: Professional studies – primary phase* (2nd edn). Exeter: Learning Matters.

Before you read the next extract prepare yourself by reading:

- Farrell, M (2001) *Standards and special educational needs*. London: Continuum.
- Florian, L (2005) 'Inclusion, 'special needs' and the search for new understandings'. *Support for Learning* 20(2): pp96–98.
- Gibson, S and Blandford, S (2005) *Managing special educational needs*. London: Paul Chapman.
- McIntyre, D (2003) 'Has classroom teaching served its day?', in Nind, M. *et al.*, *Inclusive education: diverse perspectives*. London: David Fulton.
- Soan, S (2004) (ed) *Additional educational needs – inclusive approaches to teaching*. London: David Fulton.

Extract: Dyson, A and Millward, A (2002) 'Looking them in the eyes: is rational provision for students "with special educational needs" really possible?' in Farrell, P and Ainscow, M (eds) *Making special education inclusive*. London: David Fulton.

Towards an alternative system?

It is our contention that the problems embodied in the Code are structural rather than superficial. The recent revision of the Code (DfES 2001b) has doubtless brought about a series of minor, but nonetheless important, improvements. However, it leaves the basic assumptions and processes of the 1994 Code – which themselves date back to Warnock and beyond – substantially unchanged. If we are to tackle the underlying problems of the Code, it is, we suggest, essential to question the orthodoxy of those fundamental assumptions and, particularly, the assumption that special needs provision must be based on a high level of individualisation. Undoubtedly, there are some children 'with special educational needs' whose pattern of difficulties and characteristics is complex and atypical. It may well be that assessment and provision on an individual basis is the only viable approach in such cases. However, it is also arguable that what the Warnock Report and the 1994 Code did was to generalise from this rather small population to another much larger population ('Warnock's 18 per cent') whose situation is quite different.

The majority of so-called special educational needs actually manifest themselves in a limited number of forms – mild or moderate general learning difficulties (usually in literacy), specific learning difficulties (again in literacy) and behavioural difficulties (Croll and Moses 2000; Dyson and Millward, in press). Not only are these forms of difficulty familiar in every school and LEA, but they are also reasonably well understood by both researchers and practitioners and, more important, there is a well-established repertoire of strategies for addressing them.

Indeed, there is some evidence that, as advocates of the 'whole-school approach' (Dessent 1987) were wont to suggest, that repertoire comprises no more than variations on 'good' mainstream teaching (Norwich and Lewis 2001).

With this in mind, it might make sense to recast our notion of individualisation, at least for the majority of children 'with special educational needs'. Of course, *all* children are individuals and ought to have educational experiences that are in some sense tailored to their particular characteristics. However, there is no reason why, for most children 'with special needs', such individualisation has to take the form of complex assessment processes leading to unique packages of provision. Instead, it might, as for most other children, take the form of classroom-level modifications of established approaches – the sort of 'improvisation' that, Ainscow argues, characterises good teaching (Ainscow 1995; 1997; 1999). This would then mean that the energies of the special needs system could be directed not into finding case-by-case approaches to particular configurations of learning characteristics, but into identifying and developing broad strategies for responding to commonly occurring difficulties.

This in turn implies that the task of the central Government need not be confined to issuing procedural guidance. Instead, Government should be in the business of ensuring that the best possible strategies are routinely available in schools by commissioning research and research reviews (involving practitioners, of course, as co-generators of pedagogical knowledge), by issuing substantive guidance, by managing training and by ensuring that resourcing sustains the infrastructure to support these strategies rather than 'packages' for individual students (see Meijer 1999). It would, of course, be unrealistic to expect that such a system could be entirely problem-free. However, it would hold out the prospect both of a greater comparability – and hence equity – of provision for similar needs across schools and LEAs, and of greater rationality in the sense of provision based clearly on an educational response to those needs. Above all, such a system would, we suggest, be much more likely to result in more effective provision – effective, that is, in helping children to learn – than the current localised, individualised and adhocratic hotchpotch.

A few years ago, when the Code was first introduced and, certainly, at the time of the Warnock Report (DES 1978), such a view would, no doubt, have seemed ridiculous. Given the tradition of local decision making and the known limitations of a categorical approach to special educational needs, the individualised model did indeed represent the best available alternative. Since then, however, much has changed. In particular, curriculum, pedagogy and school organisation and leadership have become significantly more centrally directed and – in some respects at least – more evidence-informed. In the light of developments such as the National Curriculum, the OFSTED frameworks, the National Literacy and Numeracy Strategies and the targeted approaches of Excellence in Cities, Sure Start and a host of other initiatives, the post-Warnock approach to special needs education is beginning to look like distinctly old technology. Now may be just the time for a new approach.

Why?

Why should we consider the emotional and social factors of learning when identifying and assessing children's individual needs?

This is an important aspect of the inclusion agenda and of special educational needs, and one that has important implications for both children and teachers. Many children, especially those with social, emotional and behavioural difficulties, may have the ability to learn, but lack positive, meaningful personal experiences that will enable them to utilise their abilities (Hanko, 2003). The identification of need is vital in this situation and it is not assessment, or at least assessment alone, that will remove the barriers to achievement. The children need to be provided with experiences by the teacher that enable them to gain a sense of:

- being valued as a person;
- belonging and involvement;
- personal satisfaction and achievement;
- being accepted and listened to;
- congruence between personal and institutional values;
- personal meaningfulness of the tasks of teaching and learning;
- efficacy, power to influence things for the better. (Hanko, 2003, p128)

Interestingly, as in all other instances, these factors are important and matter for all children and all teachers as well. Therefore to be able to identify and assess need effectively teachers should recognise the significance of their interactions with the children, because without this, assessments completed may indicate suggested areas for specific work, but fail to deal with the real issues, perhaps causing the lack of motivation and willingness to engage in learning. For the majority of children, the development of whole-school policies that foster these experiences as part of the work of the school will be sufficient to support them, enabling them to progress in their personal and social development, as well as in their learning. In this and similar situations, such a whole-school policy is known by all the teachers and will actually facilitate the identification of broad strategies to be used generally in the classroom. Hence the identification and assessment of need for a number of children previously given 'special needs' provision in the form of a separate package becomes unnecessary.

How?

How do we ensure that children with complex and severe special educational needs receive thorough assessments, yet others are not over assessed?

The *Special Educational Needs Code of Practice* (DfES, 2001b) and the *National Special Educational Needs Specialist Standards* (TTA, 1999) both provide clear guidance for class teachers and SENCOs to identify when thorough assessments are required. The legislative framework is also in place, to ensure the protection of those children who have the most severe needs and require a substantial amount of additional support and resources.

For others without *complex and atypical difficulties and characteristics* (Dyson and Millward, 2002, p21) it is the day-to-day assessments that help to inform teaching and learning, and reveals clearly to teachers how much each child has understood the learning experiences. Guidance issued by the government is encouraging using good general whole-class practice strategies for identification and assessment of need. It is considered that by using this method the class teacher has ownership of the whole process and with support and advice can try to adapt his or her teaching strategies and interventions to meet the needs of individual children, prior to requesting any formal additional assessments. Suggested effective assessment strategies (DfES, 2004a, p.15) are:

- using questions and sharing comments with children;
- making observations of children during teaching and while they work;
- holding discussions with children;
- analysing work, reporting to children and guiding their improvements;
- engaging children in the assessment process.

What?

What identification and assessment processes are therefore necessary for children with special educational needs?

You will quickly recognise and understand that for all of the children in your class there are a number of formal assessments that are required annually. For children with special educational needs it is vital that you use your skills as a practitioner to identify where they are finding it difficult to access, engage with or participate in lessons and during social activities as early as possible. Observations and discussions with the children will frequently inform you where their difficulties are occurring and you can change or differentiate your tasks and support systems accordingly. If progress is still not occurring and additional advice is sought you will have gathered vital information already that can be immediately utilised by specialists to guide and determine further assessment. In this way you are trying to identify need as early as possible, but also accessing different strategies and learning systems, prior to the request for more individualised focused assessment.

Personal response

The identification and assessment of need is a complex issue that is different for every child with special educational needs. Reflect and critically discuss with a colleague whether you feel the following statements are true or false for learners in classrooms today:

- It is important to consider all aspects of a child's life and to try to adapt your teaching practices as much as possible, before following one specific avenue of assessment.
- The process of requesting a statutory assessment is the only route to take if you want a child to receive a thorough identification and assessment of need.
- Children with special educational needs should be thoroughly assessed as soon as a 'problem' is identified.

Practical implications and activities

Children are very likely to be identified as having a special educational need at some point during their school career up until the current time. Think carefully about how you would identify and assess a child that you had observed was finding it difficult to remember instructions and information given to him verbally. Evaluate your answers using guidance and literature to support your thinking under the following headings:

- how was the need identified?
- by whom was the need identified?
- how and who assessed the barriers to learning initially?
- what action was taken as a result of that assessment?
- what happened next and who was involved?
- how did the process of identification and assessment involve and respect the wishes of: the child; the parent/carer; the teacher; the school?

2. Deliberate with a colleague whether you feel a school that is trying to develop inclusive practice should need to seek or carry out individualised assessments for children with special educational needs or not? You may give your answers corresponding to the *Special Educational Needs Code of Practice* (DfES, 2001b) levels of need, School Action, School Action Plus or a Statement of Educational Need.

Further reading

Corbett, J and Slee, R (2000) 'An international conversation on inclusive education: a connective pedagogy', in Armstrong, F, Armstrong, D and Barton, L (eds) *Inclusive education: policy, contexts and comparative perspectives*. London: David Fulton.

DfES, (2001b) *Special educational needs code of practice*. Annesley: DfES.

DfES, (2004a) *Primary National Strategy – learning and teaching for children with special educational needs in the primary years*. Annesley: DfES.

Hanko, G (2003) 'Towards an inclusive school culture – but what happened to Elton's "affective curriculum?"'. *British Journal of Special Education*, 30(3): 125–131.

Mittler, P (2000) *Working towards inclusive education: social contexts*. London: David Fulton.

O'Brien, T (2000) 'Increasing inclusion: did anyone mention learning?', *REACH. Journal of Special Needs in Ireland*, 14(1): 2–12.

Tassoni, P (2003) *Supporting special needs: understanding inclusion in the early years*. Oxford: Heinemann.

Teacher Training Agency (1999) *National special educational needs specialist standards*. London: TTA.

Thomas, G and Vaughan, M (2004) *Inclusive education – reading and reflections*. Maidenhead: OUP.

10 The provision and evaluation of need

By the end of this chapter you should have considered and reflected upon:

- **why** it was felt necessary to reconsider the systems that provided and evaluated education and support for children with special educational needs;
- **what** the future is for special educational needs;
- **how** can we ensure that children with special educational needs are provided with the most appropriate education, in a school that best meets both their educational and social requirements, to foster self-esteem, academic progress and social skills within the current climate.

Linking your learning
Achieving QTS: Professional studies primary phase, second edition, Jacques, K and Hyland, R (2003), Chapter 12.

Professional Standards for QTS
1.7, 3.2.1, 3.2.2, 3.2.3, 3.2.6, 3.2.7.

Introduction

What is considered to be 'special provision'? The *Special Educational Needs Code of Practice* (DfES, 2001b, 1.3 p 6) defines it as:

> educational provision which is additional to, or otherwise different from, the educational provision made generally for children of their age in schools maintained by the LEA, other than special schools, in the area.

It acknowledges that the *National Curriculum Inclusion Statement's* (QCA, 1999) three principles for inclusion should be applied for all children to provide the most effective learning opportunities, (DfES, 2001b, 5:19, p.47):

- setting suitable learning challenges;
- responding to pupils' diverse needs;
- overcoming potential barriers to learning and assessment for individuals and groups of pupils.

However, there are some children that may need even greater assistance, additional and different resources, and approaches to teaching, to achieve this.

It is vital, of course, to evaluate and review the effectiveness of provision for children with special educational needs and to ensure the children are making adequate progress. The *Special Educational Needs Code of Practice* (DfES, 2001b, 5:42, p. 52) suggests that adequate progress can be defined in many ways including:

- closing the attainment gap between the child and their peers;
- preventing the attainment gap growing wider;
- demonstrating improvements in the child's behaviour;
- demonstrating an improvement in self-help, social or personal skills.

You will have to be aware that although you wish to follow the *National Curriculum Inclusion Statement* (QCA, 1999) for all the children in your class, there are quite likely to be one or two whose level of need cannot be met most appropriately without additional and different teaching and/or learning environment. However, your efforts in adapting and providing a differentiated curriculum will supply a wealth of information to other professionals who are asked to carry out further additional assessments.

Before you read the following extract, prepare yourself by reading:

- DfES, (2001b) *Special educational needs code of practice*, Chapter 5, pp44–58. Annesley: DfES.
- Gross, J and White, A (2003) *Special educational needs and school improvement – practical strategies for raising standards*, Chapters 6 and 7, pp63–99. London: David Fulton.
- Horsfall, B (2004) 'Special educational needs and the teacher', in Jacques, K and Hyland, R *Achieving QTS: Professional studies, primary phase* (2nd Edn). Exeter: Learning Matters.

Extract: Dyson, A and Millward, A (2002) 'Looking them in the eyes: is rational provision for students "with special educational needs" really possible?' in Farrell, P and Ainscow, M (eds), *Making special education inclusive*. London: David Fulton. Read p13–16, section 'Introduction'.

Introduction

Children have *special educational needs* if they have a *learning difficulty* which calls for *special educational provision* to be made for them … *Special educational provision* means: … educational provision which is additional to, or otherwise different from, the educational provision made generally for children of their age in schools maintained by the LEA, other than special schools, in the area.

(1996 Education Act, section 312, as cited in the *Special Educational Needs Code of Practice*, DfES 2001b: 6)

The 1996 Act's definition of special educational needs (dating back, of course, to the recommendations of the Warnock Report, DES 1978, and beyond) rests on two assumptions that are shared by education systems across the world, which now seem so self-evident that we tend to take them for granted. The first is that there are some children who 'need' provision that is special in the sense of being 'additional to or different from' that made for other children. The second, which follows from the 'additional' or 'different' nature of special provision, is that such provision will commonly require additional resourcing and hence additional funding. In recent years, of course, there has been considerable debate about whether a separate special education system or a more unified 'inclusive' system is the best way of making provision responsive to individual differences. Nonetheless, all systems, however 'inclusive', tend to accept that children differ from each other in ways that are important for their learning, that these differences should be reflected in the provision made for them and that variations in provision will sometimes demand equivalent variations in resourcing.

It follows that education systems have to make decisions about matching provision and resources to needs. These decisions are made centrally, by national or local government officials or at school level by teachers in management positions, or at classroom level by teachers directing their time and energy towards particular students. Given that this is the case, we have suggested elsewhere (Crowther, Dyson and Millward 1998) that these decisions ought to be tested against two principles – rationality and equity. Decisions ought to be rational in that they are made for good reasons which can be explained and defended in educational terms; and they ought to be equitable in that they result in just treatment for individual children, for instance, by matching the form of provision and level of resources to some notion of the differing levels and forms of 'needs'.

In England (and, to varying degrees, in the rest of the UK), we have had since 1944 two formal systems for decision making of this kind. The 1944 Education Act consolidated a *categorical* system of special education, based on the assumption that skilled professionals notably doctors and psychologists could 'ascertain' (in the language of the time) children's difficulties in terms of a series of 'categories of handicap'. On the basis of this ascertainment, children could then be placed in institutions where specialist provision for that sort of difficulty was available. In practice, this tended (though not invariably) to entail placement in special schools – for the 'educationally subnormal', the 'maladjusted', those with 'physical handicaps' and so on.

In the years leading up to the Warnock Report (DES 1978), this system increasingly came to seem less rational and equitable (Stakes and Horriby 1997): children's difficulties did not fit neatly into the categories; arbitrary decisions had to be made to include or exclude 'borderline' children within the categories; formally recognised types of provision tended to be in separate institutions; and 'excluded' children received no formal protection for whatever provision they might or might not receive. Warnock's response was to call for a different system of decision making – a call that was heeded in the 1981 Education Act and that has formed the basis of the statutory special education system ever since. Instead of allocating children to categories, their 'special educational needs' were to be assessed on an *individual* basis, taking into account not only the sometimes complex pattern of individual difficulties but, to some extent at least, the particular educational context within which those difficulties arose. Following this assessment, provision could be made to meet the needs of particular individuals in particular settings. This might still involve placement in specialist institutions, but might equally involve the formulation of individualised 'packages' of provision in ordinary schools, each one resourced differently from the next.

This more individualised system was potentially more sensitive both to individual differences and to contextual factors. However, this sensitivity came at a cost. The categorical system offered the prospect (whatever the reality) that children with similar difficulties in different parts of the country would be assessed and allocated to categories against similar diagnostic criteria and would then be placed in broadly similar types of specialist institution. The new system offered no such guarantees. The more individualised assessment and provision was, the more difficult it became to compare case with case. In practice, provision resulted from a complex interplay of different types of professional advice – educational psychologists, teachers, doctors and others – different (and often conflicting) interests – those of the parents, of the school and of the LEA – all set within the context of a highly variable local pattern of provision and local expectations of what mainstream schools would and should provide.

What finally set light to this tinder box was the far reaching package of reforms introduced in the late 1980s and early 1990s, notably the 1988 Education Reform Act. Although few of these reforms had much explicitly to say about special needs education, their impact was significant. As has often been argued (see, for instance, Bines 1995; Bowers 1995; Gold, Bowe and Ball 1993; Riddell and Brown 1994; Rouse and Florian 1997), these reforms created a situation in which many mainstream schools sought either to rid themselves of students who presented difficulties or to educate them only if extra resources were available. The statutory assessment procedures introduced by the 1981 Act gave LEAs a set of procedures which they could, in principle, use to control the rising tide of referrals. However, nowhere had Government set down any criteria determining which children, with which sorts and levels of needs should receive which sorts of provision. In the face of mounting pressure from schools, parents and lobby groups, LEAs could only advance the outcomes of individualised (and hence, non-comparable) assessments together with eminently contestible local custom and practice. Not surprisingly, rates of statementing began to rise alarmingly (DfEE 1997), with the imminent threat that LEAs' special needs responsibilities would wreck their budgets (Coopers and Lybrand 1996). At the same time, a series of official reports expressed deep concern about both the quality and the efficiency of special needs education as it had developed under the somewhat laissez-faire arrangements of the post-1981 period (DES 1989a, 1989b; HMI 1990a, 1990b; Audit Commission and HMI 1992a, 1992b). It is in this context that the first SEN Code of Practice (DFE 1994) was introduced.

At the time, the Code was given a cautiously positive welcome right across the special needs community (see, for instance, Dyer 1995; Dyson, Lin and Millward 1996; Garner 1996; Lewis, Neill and Campbell 1996; Russell 1994). Despite its somewhat bureaucratic appearance, it did at least raise the profile of special needs education in mainstream schools, systematise procedures, and offer some additional guarantees to students and their parents. However, the Code can also be understood as an attempt to regain control over the growth in spending on special needs education. The five-stage assessment procedure, in particular, put pressure on schools to meet children's 'special needs' out of their delegated budgets *before* requesting further resources from the LEA.

In effect, the stages constituted an extension of the 'Warnock' statutory assessment procedures to children in mainstream schools with much lower levels of need. The essential format was the same – an individualised assessment, drawing on a range of perspectives (class teacher, Special Educational Needs Coordinator (SENCO), support service member and so on), informing and involving parents and leading on to similarly individualised provision. The principle of matching provision to need at school level was clear enough. However, the very fact that these procedures had so much in common with their statutory counterparts raised the possibility that they might be no more effective in controlling demand, let alone in ensuring equity of provision.

This possibility became even more significant when, in 1997, the incoming 'New' Labour Government committed itself to the development of a more 'inclusive' education system (DfEE 1997; 1998). Since this move involved mainstream schools in accepting greater responsibility for a wider range of students, it inevitably entailed some clarification of the respective contributions to provision made by schools and LEAs. As part of a wider review of the working of the SEN Code of Practice, therefore, the Government resolved to issue guidance as to the criteria that might be used in deciding how to relate children's 'needs' to the forms of action that might be taken and the levels of provision that might be made by schools and LEAs. That guidance was ultimately issued alongside the draft revised Code as the *Thresholds* document (DfEE 2000), and some of the essentials of this work were subsequently incorporated into the SEN Code of Practice 2001 (DfES 2001b) and the non-statutory *SEN Toolkit* (DfES 2001a). The study that is reported in the remainder of this chapter is intended to provide an evidential basis for this guidance.

Why?

Why is provision an important issue for schools, when considering the children who have special educational needs?

With accountability and self-evaluation an essential aspect of the school cycle currently, it is imperative that special educational needs plays its full role in this. At the whole school level it is really necessary to write a plan or map for the provision the school will make available for children with special educational needs and also disabilities, in addition to the school improvement plan. This provision cycle should run alongside the whole school improvement plan, taking into consideration factors such as self-evaluation and budgets. You clearly should be aware of this to understand how the school will support the children with special educational needs and how decisions are made. This type of approach can also assist in planning for additional adult support in classrooms. As a consequence of reviewing provision and completing a self-evaluation cycle, the identification of where support staff are really required to ensure children with special educational needs receive the best support can be prioritised.

Another factor of the whole school evaluation of special educational needs provision is the analysis of the pupils' needs to see if there are trends or indicators of specific forms of provision to be required within the following year or two. This can help with planning for training, INSET and specialised forms of resources or programmes such as symbol work, for children with speech, language and communication needs or autism, for example.

Finally it is considered that if children with special educational needs are well catered for and well taught, then it will also have a positive effect on all children, as good practice is beneficial for all.

What?

What do you need to consider when providing and evaluating learning and teaching for children with special educational needs?

Having written a provision map or plan to support whole school special educational needs, this same tool can help guide, monitor and evaluate the learning and teaching for individual children. A teacher needs to be able to evaluate how a child with special educational needs accesses learning most efficiently, how much individualised support – whether in the form of a teaching assistant or an individualised approach to the curriculum – is necessary and also needs to have good monitoring systems. This approach enables provision to be mapped from year to year and individual difficulties can often be identified using this information at an early stage. An individual teacher can monitor the effect of provision and identify when it is inappropriate or ineffectual. Therefore you will need to consider factors such as:

- what level of support the child requires;
- how best to provide the support;
- what equipment/resources are necessary;
- how you can most effectively plan for the individual need;
- what training you or a teaching assistant requires to be able to engage with the child's needs.

How?

How important is it for you to have a knowledge and understanding of the difficulties children may experience?

Many experienced mainstream school teachers say that they find it very hard to identify what problem a child may have. They will know the child has a problem, but may well be unable to locate the main cause of the difficulty and hence additional or different provision put in place, is quite likely to be inappropriate. Thus having a broad understanding and knowledge of special educational needs is very beneficial, but as a new teacher you will be able to seek the advice of the SENCO who will be able to help you with identifying, providing for and evaluating the effectiveness of the provision and progress made for individual children.

Personal response

1. In the past providing for children with special educational needs has tended to be very ad hoc. Using the literature suggested and current government guidance, reflect on how a more formalised approach to planning for provision on an annual basis will support schools, and hence individual children with special educational needs. This is a complex issue that has many controversial factors.
2. Discuss with a colleague how influential (a) finance (b) staffing (c) expertise and (d) a child's learning and social needs, will be in setting targets on the provision map or plan of a school. Then critically evaluate how this approach, recognising that it will be part of the self-evaluation process for the whole school, will positively or negatively effect special educational needs provision for individual children.

Practical implications and activities

When planning a lesson for a mainstream class, including children with a whole range of special educational needs, how do you to decide what strategies to use and how to differentiate your tasks? What information do you need prior to the planning stage that helps you make these decisions? What other factors are important?

Reflect on your answers carefully, questioning how you make your decisions and whether this method(s) is based on good practice, sound understanding of the needs of individual children or the availability of resources, human and material.

Further reading

Constable, D (2002) *Planning and organising the SENCO Year*. London: David Fulton.

Cowne, E (1998) (2nd edn), *The SENCO handbook*. London: David Fulton.

Wall, K (2003) *Special needs and early years*. Chapter 6, pp111–131. London: Paul Chapman.

Before you read the next extract prepare yourself by reading:

- DfES (2004) *Removing barriers to achievement*, Chapter 3, pp52–68. Annesley: DfES.
- DfES (2004a) *Primary National Strategy – learning and teaching for children with special educational needs in the primary years*. Annesley: DfES.

Extract: Florian, L, Rouse, M, Black-Hawkins, K and Jull, S (2004) 'What can national data sets tell us about inclusion and pupil achievement?' *British Journal of Special Education*, **31(3): 115–121. Read pp117–118.**

So what is a special educational need?
The term 'special educational needs' covers an array of difficulties as highlighted in the 2001 *Special Educational Needs Code of Practice* which:

> 'does not assume that there are hard and fast categories of special educational need … [and] recognises that there is a wide spectrum of special educational needs that are frequently inter-related, although there are also specific needs that usually relate directly to particular types of impairment.'
>
> (DfES, 2001a, p.85, para. 7.52)

Some argue that classroom teachers should take responsibility for providing the necessary support to help pupils overcome barriers to learning with specialist input as needed; others believe that specialists should work directly with learners; still others argue that specialist facilities are the best way to provide for some special educational needs. As a result, numerous approaches to provision have been developed and the extent to which these require a designation of special educational needs is variable. Moreover, variations in context produce different ideas about who has special needs. A child who is experiencing difficulties in learning to read may have a Statement for dyslexia in one LEA but not in another. In addition it would be unwise to compare the progress of two pupils with a Statement of Special Educational Needs where one has a Statement because of profound and multiple learning difficulties and the other has a Statement for a specific learning difficulty.

The reintroduction of categories of special educational needs

In response to the lack of specificity in special educational needs data, the PLASC data set was amended in 2004 to include the 12 categories currently used by OFSTED (see Table 1). The adoption of these categories may lead to more detailed, but not necessarily more consistent, information about which students, described as having 'special educational needs', are included in which schools. Therefore, patterns of provision may become more clearly identifiable, within and across schools. For example, rather than describing one school as being 'more inclusive' than another (because of the number of students, with 'special educational needs' as a proportion of numbers of students on roll), the PLASC will, in theory, be able to identify which schools are most able to include which 'types' of 'special educational needs' as well as being able to identify gaps and anomalies in provision.

A consequence of increasing the number of categories of 'special educational needs' may lead to less consistency rather than more. Such a system will inevitably be subject to inaccuracy and oversimplification in ways that other categories used in PLASC, such as age and gender, are not. For example, a student who is female and aged 12–13 continues to be female and aged 12–13 for the course of a school year. If her family circumstances change and she become eligible for free school meals, then that change is a precise one (she either is or is not eligible to receive free school meals, even if the circumstances leading to the change may differ from student to student). Any errors in these aspects of the data are likely to be caused by the introduction of an error at the point of entering the data, rather than by fundamental difficulties arising from the use of imprecise categories. Educational needs cannot be easily determined; they are changeable, open to interpretation and very often context-specific. Even assigning pupils to one of the listed ethnic groups may prove to be problematic, as schools have to report the ethnic designation selected by parents or the pupils themselves.

Table 1: Categories of special educational needs

1. Specific learning disability (SpLD)
2. Moderate learning difficulty (MLD)
3. Severe learning difficulty (SLD)
4. Profound and multiple learning difficulty (PMLD)
5. Emotional and behavioural difficulty (EBD)
6. Speech, language and communication needs (SLCN)
7. Hearing impairment (HI)
8. Visual impairment (VI)
9. Multi-sensory impairment (MSI)
10. Physical difficulty (PD)
11. Autism spectrum disorder (ASD)
12. Other (OTH)

Some of these difficulties are already apparent in the consultation document *Classification of special educational needs* (DfES, 2003b), which states: 'We are asking for pupils' greatest/primary and secondary needs.' Therefore, comparisons between individual pupils and groups of pupils on the basis of their 'special educational needs' will not be straightforward. For example, what does it mean to describe a student as having 'moderate learning difficulties' as a primary need and 'emotional and behavioural difficulties' as a secondary need, rather than the other way round?

The crucial question is, to what extent will attempts to produce greater specificity about the nature of children's needs be possible and helpful? It could be argued that the classification of students by 'types' of 'special educational needs' may be considered regressive, because doing so may:

- lead to increased labelling;
- herald a return to deficit notions of disability by promoting the notion that the 'fault' is in the student rather than being an artefact of the interaction between the student and the learning context;
- encourage professionals to ignore the interactive and contextual aspects of teaching and learning;
- oversimplify the complexity of children's difficulties by forcing staff to identify a primary cause of special educational need.

The (re)introduction of such categories may reify the notion of 'special educational needs', militating against a flexible and interactive approach to developing strategies to support the participation and learning of all students in schools. Such categories may encourage too strong a focus on the present 'failures' or 'problems' experienced by students rather than on their future possibilities and achievements. Further, it is likely to increase the numbers of children who are incorrectly classified, in part because the guidance to schools on how to allocate children is somewhat vague.

So is a school with a high number of pupils with special educational needs an inclusive school?

In addition to the difficulties discussed above, there is a need to differentiate between schools that have a high proportion of pupils designated as having special educational needs and inclusive schools. The concept of inclusion is not straightforward. There are numerous ways of approaching inclusive education for pupils with special educational needs. One, as evidenced by the *Index for Inclusion* (Booth, Ainscow, Black-Hawkins, Vaughan & Shaw, 2000), calls for the restructuring of mainstream schools to ensure that they are more responsive to pupil diversity. Such an approach adopts a school improvement perspective that focuses on expanding a school's capacity to respond to all its pupils. A different approach to inclusion might be called the 'special education approach' in which the pupils, staff, expertise, resources and facilities previously located in special schools are reconfigured in ways that connect to mainstream schools, for example, through dual placements or outreach initiatives (Rose & Coles, 2002). There is also a 'participation approach' to inclusion (Lunt & Norwich, 1999) which focuses on increased participation in mainstream settings linked, as Florian (1998) has argued, to ideas of active involvement and choice. Beginning with the Green Paper, *Excellence for All*

Children (DfEE, 1997), and continuing in more recent policy documents, the Government has acknowledged that there is no single best route to inclusion. Thus, a relatively high or low proportion of pupils designated as having special educational needs may be as much a function of historical patterns of provision as it is a consequence of inclusion policy or, indeed, inclusive practice. The number of pupils designated as having special educational needs within a school cannot, therefore, necessarily tell us very much about inclusion.

Technical issues

Special educational needs status

The DfES has, for many years, routinely collected data on special educational needs but changes in policy and practice regarding the identification and assessment of pupils with special educational needs have resulted in changes to the types of data that are collected. Currently, information on individual pupils relates to four 'levels' of special educational needs as described by the revised *Special Educational Needs Code of Practice* (DfES, 2001a). Previously, pupils were categorised according to a five-staged assessment process. Both systems are considered to provide a crude indicator of level of need. Further, the new data are not directly comparable to the old data because the new categories do not map neatly onto the previous system as can be seen in Table 2.

Table 2: Special educational needs status

Former Code of Practice indicators	Revised Code of Practice indicators
Stage 1 Register of special educational needs	N No special provision
Stage 2 Individual education plan	A School action
Stage 3 Assessment	P School action plus
Stage 4 Statutory assessment	Q School action plus and statutory assessment
Stage 5 Statement of Special Educational Needs	S Statement of Special Educational Needs

Over time, this anomaly will be resolved but, at present, retrospective comparisons are difficult. The fact that it is not possible, in the current data sets, to determine when a child was designated as having special educational needs compounds the problematic qualities of the data.

In addition, many LEAs have been working to reduce the numbers of Statements of Special Educational Needs that are issued by delegating funds directly to schools through a variety of mechanisms that allocate additional resources to schools through moderated panels or clusters arrangements. One consequence of this trend is that younger children are less likely to have Statements than are older children whose Statements continue to be maintained. Therefore simple comparisons about the level of need within a school, based upon the number of children with Statements, are likely to be less meaningful than the numbers in a database might suggest.

Why?

Why is it necessary to evaluate provision regularly for children with special educational needs?

First it must be said that this is important for every child. However, when additional and different provision is given to a child with special educational needs, it is a teacher's responsibility to ensure that it does actually enable the child to better access, engage with and participate in curriculum learning. If you find that particular provision is not supporting a child's learning productively, then you need to have the confidence to evaluate it and, following consultation with other colleagues, change it using the information gathered for the evaluation to inform further intervention. Without effective evaluation procedures children can be given programmes of work and support which are inappropriate, leading to a widening rather than a narrowing of the gap between peers, and limited progress.

What?

What are categories of special educational needs useful for?

The extract you have just read clearly identifies the lack of consistency regarding categories of need and provision across the country. The government want children wherever they live to have equal access to provision, but how is this going to be achieved? All children are different and therefore, although categories may be useful as identifying for teachers the primary area of need on initial investigations, the complexity of children's needs they are now having to cope with on a daily basis, will not be assisted by a list of 12 or more, categories. On many occasions I know I have had to complete assessments nearly on a 'heads or tails' response and this is clearly not a satisfactory way of making decisions for a child's future.

How?

How can consistency of provision across the country be achieved?

The government, on the second page of the new SEN strategy (DfES, 2004, Introduction) states that personalised learning is the way forward, making the necessity for categories of need unwarranted. The government see this as the way forward to improve learning:

> This strategy aims to personalise learning for all children, to make education more innovative and responsive to the diverse needs of individual children, so reducing our reliance on separate SEN structures and processes and raising the achievement of the many children ...who are considered to have SEN.

Alongside additional training, school self-evaluation, listening to the voice of the child, parental partnership and inclusion, it is envisaged that this will improve consistency of provision for all children with special educational needs in the country. Indeed the five key components of personalised learning (Last, 2004) also have the same emphasis:

- assessment for learning;
- teaching and learning strategies;
- curriculum entitlement and choice;
- a student-centred approach to school organisation;
- strong partnership beyond the school.

Personal response

1. Critically consider what skills you will need as a teacher to provide for all the diverse needs you may encounter in the classroom.
2. Do you feel a list of special educational needs categories would help you in any way? If so how? If not, why not? Discuss with a colleague how this will impact on your planning and assessments?

Practical implications and activities

Reflect on the following statement:

Without a separate system for the provision and evaluation of need for children with special educational needs, they will have to, yet again, make do with what teachers and schools have time and resources to provide. Government intention may have its heart in the right place, but is it feasible in practice?

As a new teacher entering the profession, evaluate this statement and critically review who may have been speaking and why it could have been said. Use theory and literature to support your answers. Explore the separate issues highlighted within this statement and examine their factual correctness.

Further reading

Farrell, M (2001) *Standards and special educational needs*. London: Continuum.

Florian, L *et al.* (2004) 'What can national data sets tell us about inclusion and pupil achievement?'. *British Journal of Special Education*. 31(3): 115–121.

Gibson, S and Blandford, S (2005) *Managing special educational needs*. London: Paul Chapman.

Last, G (2004) *Personalising learning: adding value to the learning journey through the primary school*. London: DfES.

Nind, M *et al.* (2003), *Inclusive education: diverse perspectives*. London: David Fulton.

Soan, S (2004) (ed) *Additional educational needs – inclusive approaches to teaching*. London: David Fulton.

References

Allan, J (2003) 'Productive pedagogies and the challenge of inclusion'. *British Journal of Special Education*, 30(4): 175–9. Blackwell Publishing on behalf of NASEN

Armstrong, D (1995) *Power and partnership in education*. London: Routledge.

Armstrong, F (1998) 'Curricula, "management" and special and inclusive education', pp48–77, in Clough, P (ed) *Managing inclusive education – from policy to experience*. London: Paul Chapman.

Armstrong, F Armstrong, D and Burton, L (eds) (2000) *Inclusive education – policy, contexts and comparative perspectives*. London: David Fulton.

Beveridge, S (2005) *Children, families and schools: developing partnerships for inclusive education*. London: Routledge Falmer.

Blamires, M and Moore, J (2003) *Support services and mainstream schools: a guide for working together*. London: David Fulton.

Blandford, S (2005a) *Sonia Blandford's Masterclass*. London: Sage.

Blandford, S (2005b) *Remodelling schools: workforce reform*. London: Pearson.

Booth, T and Ainscow, M (2002) *Index for inclusion*. Bristol: CSIE.

Bronfenbrenner, U (1970) *Two worlds of childhood: US and USSR*. New York: Sage.

Byers, R (1999) 'The National Literacy Strategy and pupils with special educational needs'. *British Journal of Special Education*, 26(1), 8–11.

CACE (1967) Plowden Report: '*Children and their Primary Schools*': Report of the Central Advisory Council for Education (England) under the Chairmanship of Lady Plowden. HMSO.

Carnie, F (2005) *Pathways to child friendly schools: a guide for parents*. HSE.

Constable, D (2002) *Planning and organising the SENCO Year*. London: David Fulton.

Corbett, J (1999) 'Inclusive education and school culture'. *International Journal of Inclusive Education*, 3(1): 53–61. Blackwell Publishing on behalf of NASEN

Corbett, J (2001) 'Teaching approaches which support inclusive education: a connective pedagogy'. *British Journal of Special Education*, 28(2): 55–59.

Corbett, J and Norwich, B (1999) 'Learners with special educational needs', in Mortimore, P (ed) *Understanding pedagogy and its impact on learning*. London: Paul Chapman.

Corbett, J and Slee, R (2000) 'An international conversation on inclusive education: a connective pedagogy', in Armstrong, F., Armstrong, D and Barton, L (eds) *Inclusive education: policy, contexts and comparative perspectives*. London: David Fulton.

Cowne, E (2002) *The SENCO handbook – working within a whole-school approach*, (2nd edn). London: David Fulton.

Croll, P and Moses, D (2000) 'Ideologies and utopias: education professionals' views of inclusion'. *European Journal of Special Needs Education*, 15(1): 1–12.

Crozier, G and Reay, D (2005) *Activating participation*. Stoke on Trent: Trentham Books Ltd.

Dessent, T (1987–8) 'Making the ordinary school special', pp77–83, in Thomas, G and Vaughan, M (2004) *Inclusive education – readings and reflections*. Maidenhead: OUP.

DfEE. (1994), *The organisation of special educational provision*. Annesley: *Circular 6.94*, DfEE.

DfES, (2001a) *Inclusive schooling: children with special educational needs*. Annesley: DfES.

DfES, (2001b) *Special educational needs code of practice*. Annesley: DfES.

DfES, (2001c) *SEN toolkit, section 1: principles and policies, Section 11 and 12*. Annesley: DfES.

DfES, (2004) *Removing barriers to achievement – the government's strategy for SEN*. Annesley: DfES.

DfES, (2004a) *Primary National Strategy – learning and teaching for children with special educational needs in the primary years*. Annesley: DfES.

DfES (2004b) *Teaching strategies and approaches for pupils with special educational needs*. Research Report RR516.

Disability Rights Commission (2002) *Code of practice for schools – Disability Discrimination Act 1995: Part 4*. London: The Stationery Office.

Dyson, A (2001) 'Special needs in the twenty-first century: where we've been and where we're going'. *British Journal of Special Education* 28(1): 27–28. Read section: 'Coming to terms with the future'.

Economic and Social Research Council (2004) *Personalised learning*. ESRC.

Farrell, M (2001) *Standards and special educational needs*. London: Continuum.

Farrell, P (2001) 'Special education in the last twenty years: have things really got better?' In *British Journal of Special Education*, 28(1): 3–9. Blackwell Publishing on behalf of NASEN

Farrell, P and Ainscow, M (eds) (2002) *Making special education inclusive*. London: David Fulton.

Florian, L *et al*. (2004) 'What can national data sets tell us about inclusion and pupil achievement?' *British Journal of Special Education*. 31(3): 115–121.

Florian, L (2005) Inclusion, 'special needs' and the search for new understandings. *Support for Learning*, 20(2): 96–98.

Frankl, C (2005) 'Managing individual education plans: reducing the load of the special educational needs coordinator'. *Support for Learning*, 20(2): 77–82.

Garner, P and Davies, J (2001) *Introducing special educational needs – a guide for students*. London: David Fulton.

Gibson, S and Blandford, S (2005) *Managing special educational needs*, pp14–22. London: Paul Chapman.

Golder, G, Norwich, B and Bayliss, P (2005) 'Preparing teachers to teach pupils with special educational needs in more inclusive schools: evaluating a PGCE development'. *British Journal of Special Education*, 32(2): 92–99. Blackwell Publishing on behalf of NASEN

Gross, J and White, A (2003) *Special educational needs and school improvement – practical strategies for raising standards*. London: David Fulton.

Greenwood, C (2002) *Understanding the needs of parents: guidelines for effective collaboration with parents of children with special educational needs*. London: David Fulton.

Hanam, D (2003) 'Participation and responsible action for all students', in *Teaching citizenship*, (Spring, 2003). Association for Citizenship Teaching.

Hanko, G (2003) 'Towards an inclusive school culture – but what happened to Elton's "affective curriculum"?'. *British Journal of Special Education*, 30(3): 125–31.

Headington, R (2000) *Monitoring, assessment, recording, reporting and accountability – meeting the standards*. London: David Fulton.

HMSO (2003) *Every child matters*. Norwich: The Stationery Office.

Horsfall, B (2004) 'Special educational needs and the teacher', in Jacques, K and Hyland, R *Achieving QTS: professional studies – primary phase*. Exeter: Learning Matters.

Jarvis, J, Iantaffi, A and Sinka, I (2003) 'Inclusion in mainstream classrooms: experiences of deaf pupils', pp206–218, in Nind *et al*. *Inclusive Education: Diverse Perspectives*. London: David Fulton.

Jones, P (2005) 'Inclusion: lessons from the children'. *British Journal of Special Education*, 32(2): 60–65. Blackwell Publishing on behalf of NASEN

Lacey, P (2001) *Support partnerships: collaboration in action*. London: David Fulton.

Last, G (2004) *Personalising learning: adding value to the learning journey through the primary school*. London: DfES.

Lindsay, G (2003) 'Inclusive education: a critical perspective'. *British Journal of Special Education*, 30(1): pp3–12. Blackwell Publishing on behalf of NASEN

Lochrie, M (2005) 'Minister must now build on family foundations' in *Times Educational Supplement*, May 20, 2005: 24.

McIntyre, D (2003) 'Has classroom teaching served its day', in Nind, M *et al*. *Inclusive education: diverse perspectives*. London: David Fulton.

Mittler, P (2000) *Working towards inclusive education: social contexts*. London: David Fulton.

Moore, J (1999) 'Developing a local authority response to inclusion'. *Support for Learning*. 14(4): 174–178.

Nind, M *et al*. (2003) *Inclusive education: diverse perspectives*. London: David Fulton.

Norwich, B and Lewis, A (2004) 'How specialized is teaching pupils with disabilities and difficulties?', in Lewis, A and Norwich, B (eds) *Special teaching for special children? – pedagogies for inclusion*. Maidenhead: OUP.

O'Brien, T (2000) 'Increasing inclusion: did anyone mention learning?', *REACH. Journal of Special Needs in Ireland*, 14(1): 2–12.

O'Brien, T (2001) *Enabling inclusion: blue skies . . . dark clouds?* London: Optimus Publishing.

QCA (1999) *The National Curriculum inclusion statement*, 458. Sudbury: QCA.

Riddell, S (2000) 'Inclusion and choice: mutually exclusive principles in special educational needs', pp118–119, in Armstrong, F, Armstrong, D and Barton, L (eds) *Inclusive education – policy, contexts and comparative perspectives*. London: David Fulton.

Rix, J (2003) 'A parent's wish-list', in Nind, M, Rix, J, Sheehy, K and Simmons, K (eds) *Inclusive education: diverse perspectives*. London: David Fulton in association with The Open University.

Roaf, C (2002) *Coordinating services for included children: joined up action*. Buckingham: Open University Press.

Soan, S (2004) (ed) *Additional educational needs – inclusive approaches to teaching*. London: David Fulton.

South East Region SEN Partnership (undated) *Working positively with parents*. Filsham Valley School: Michael Phillips.

Tassoni, P (2003) *Supporting special needs: understanding inclusion in the early years*. Oxford: Heinemann.

Teacher Training Agency (1998) *National standards for special educational needs co-ordinators*. London: TTA.

Teacher Training Agency (1999) *National special educational needs specialist standards*. London: TTA.

Teaching and Learning Research Programme (2004) *Personalised learning – a commentary by the teaching and learning research programme*. Economic and Social Research Council. **www.tlrp.org**

Thacker, J, Strudwick, D and Babbedge, E (2002) *Educating children with emotional and behavioural difficulties – inclusive practice in mainstream schools*. London: Routledge Falmer.

Thomas, G and Vaughan, M (2004) *Inclusive education – reading and reflections*. Maidenhead: OUP.

UNESCO (1994) *The UNESCO Salamanca Statement and framework for action on special needs education*. Paris: UNESCO.

Vincent, C (2004) *Including parents*. Berkshire: Open University.

Weatherley, R A and Lipsky, M (1977) 'Street-level bureaucrats', pp47–50, in Thomas, G and Vaughan, M (2004) (eds) *Inclusive Education – readings and reflections*. Maidenhead: OUP.

Wedell, K (2000) 'Putting 'inclusion' into practice. Points from the SENCO-Forum'. *British Journal of Special Education*, 27(2): 100.

Index